Third Edition
THE INSTANT BUSINESS PLAN BOOK

12 *Quick-and-Easy* Steps to a Profitable Business

by Gustav Berle, Ph.D. and Paul Kirschner

PUMA PUBLISHING COMPANY
Santa Maria, California

Copyright © 1994, 1997, 2000

Puma Publishing Company

Santa Maria, California
All Rights Reserved

First Printing January 1994
Second Printing (Revised) January 1997
Third Printing May 1998
Fourth Printing (Revised) June 1999
Fifth Printing (Revised) January 2000

Library of Congress Cataloging-in-Publication Data

Berle, Gustav, 1920-
    The instant business plan book: 12 quick-and-easy steps to a profitable business/by
Gustav Berle and Paul Kirschner. — 3rd ed.

        p. cm.
Includes index.
ISBN 0-940673-90-8 — ISBN 0-940673-42-8 (softcover)
    1. Business planning. 2. Small business – Management. 3. Business enterprises – Finance.
4. Success in Business. I. Kirschner, Paul, 1917-   . II. Title.

HD30.28 .B455 2000
658.4'012–dc21   99-058918

ABOUT THE AUTHORS

Paul Kirschner has traveled throughout the U.S. giving seminars on business plan preparations for units of the SBA, Department of Defense, Department of Agriculture, and Department of Labor. He was former director of SCORE/SBA, commandant of a 1,500-student Army Reserve School and taught college-level army courses. He has been an analyst of more than 100 diverse small business operations and counseled over 1,000 clients. His career includes managing and controlling manufacturing firms grossing from $500,000 to $25 million, and working with manufacturers in the Far East, Latin America, Russia, Hungary, Kenya, Egypt, the Caribbean and China.

Gustav Berle died in late 1996 at the age 76. We will miss him dearly. He authored *Retiring to Your Own Business* and *The International Instant Business Plan*, both published by Puma Publishing, Inc., as well as ten other books for Wiley, McGraw-Hill and Prentice-Hall. Berle taught at Florida International University and had a Ph.D. in business administration. He was formerly National Marketing Director of SCORE/SBA, as well as a publisher, editor and public relations consultant.

ACKNOWLEDGMENTS

Special thanks are due to the directors and officials of the U.S Department of Commerce and the U.S. Small Business Administration; to Bill Valenta for his suggested changes which greatly improved this book; to Robert Howard for his fine cover design, and to Elaine at Graphics Limited. As usual, Curt Scott of Crown Publishing went beyond the call of duty to design and edit these pages. His devotion to excellence is rare these days. Alex Grossman of SCORE provided valuable new material included in this edition.

TABLE OF CONTENTS

INTRODUCTION

During the past few years the use of a business plan in starting a small business or making application for a business loan has become requisite. This trend has been accepted virtually all over the commercial world.

Having a business plan is good for the entrepreneur as well. Without it the business person might be traveling in a strange land without a road map. The problem is not with the acceptance and the logic of the business plan, but with the assumed complexity of it. It need not be complicated, however.

In Germany, France, England, Russia, Italy, Latin America or Scandinavia the need of a business plan is the same. Business is conducted in almost every country in a similar manner. Money is needed and money is borrowed in every country under similar circumstances— you ask for a certain amount, you offer proof of your need, you present the lender with security or collateral, you make arrangements to pay back the loan and you pay interest.

The preparation and presentation of a business plan details the need and offers proof of the borrower's viability and ability to repay the loan. It also shows that the entrepreneur is a professional, is serious about running the business, and has prepared well. This book will show you the way—with a minimum of confusion, double talk and unnecessary detail.

In this book the authors are making two assumptions:
1. that you are a small-business person who wants to go into an enterprise of your own, expand a business you already own, or want to borrow money from either a personal or commercial source; and
2. that you have a general idea that a business plan is desirable, even

With your business plan, you become a professional.

necessary (if you are going for a loan), but that you need more guidance and specific help.

There is rarely one single way of preparing a business plan. However, there are some specific ground rules that the authors have developed. In this book they have narrowed down the why and how of preparing a business plan into 12 easy steps.

What Is a Business Plan Anyway?

Your blueprint. Your map. Your statement of plans and hopes. Your compass. Your guidepost or guidelines to planned action. Your business philosophy backed by realism. Your current and futuristic X-ray of your business. Your reminder system. It is all of these and more. In a previous book, *The Small Business Information Handbook*, author Gustav Berle offers the following detailed explanation:

"To plan and operate a successful business, it has always been necessary to have a business plan. In recent years it has emerged as a major topic of business talk, as if it were a unique discovery. What is a business plan? It is your guidepost for your business's existence, your roadmap that shows you how to go forward on your road to success, your blueprint for building your enterprise, and the key that can open the door to your bank loan. Without a viable, complete, credible business plan, as an owner you are groping in the maze of entrepreneurship. With your business plan, you become a professional. It can lead to riches, or it can reveal to you pitfalls that you have ignored. Revealed pitfalls are not unconquerable stumbling blocks—they are incentives for you to do more research, learn more, do more checking, rein-in enthusiasm until your knowledge catches up with it. Your business plan is the heart of your business's start."

You can aid the survival rate by developing a business plan

You need a business plan:
- when you want to start a new business;
- when you want to correct a losing trend;
- when you want to expand a business;
- when you want to sell or pass on a business;
- when you want to get a loan.

The latter reason is generally thought to be the most important one, even though in practice it is not. The most important consideration especially when you are asking for somebody else's money, is management—in short: YOU.

We will cover the "You Factor" later in the book. Here we will consider the first reason as the one that most entrepreneurs need a business plan. Again, a couple of reasons man date this emphasis. For one, many new companies are incorporated each year, and perhaps twice as many just start up a business as a sole proprietorship or partnership, with the legal umbrella known as a "corporation"; abbreviations that signify corporate limited-liability status include *"Inc.," "Corp.,"* and *"Ltd.,"* as well as *"GmbH"* (German for *Gesellschaft mit beschränkter Haftung,* which means, quite literally, "company with limited liability"), *N.V.* (Dutch for *Naamloze Vennootschap*) and *"SpA"* (Italian). It is at start up that a business plan is most vital, and here is where we'll cast our spot light. At the genesis of a new business, we sometimes need to pull on the balloon string to bring the airborne, free-spirited sphere back to earth a bit.

Business ideas are often generated over the breakfast table, while lolling on a beach during a vacation break, or at a moment of frustration with the status quo. This idea is then developed into an embryo with further discussion and research, soul-searching and questioning. The formation of the fetus, the final stage before birth, becomes then a matter of intense activity. Unfortunately, business starts, unlike the majority of births, do not have a definite gestation period. Some businesses are stillborn or do not survive through adolescence. Those that mature into adulthood after five years amount to a bare 20 percent. We can aid the survival rate by developing a business plan. But instead of thinking of the business plan as a lifesaver to be tossed to us by a banker or business consultant, why not use it to construct the business from the start, along sound and firm lines?

Checklist of Information Needed For A Complete Business Plan

Type of business or service: You must have training or experience in the type of business under consideration. You cannot hire a person who has the experience you lack, in hopes that his or her knowledge will make the business go.

Capital: It takes money to start your business. Borrowing money is possible, but only if you have sufficient funds of your own in cash, inventory and/or equipment to provide a reasonable equity for loan consideration. Sufficient funds should be available to meet overhead and take advantage of discounts. You'll also need the ability to arrange credit to handle unexpected financial challenges.

Location: Space leased or owned must be sufficient to meet the needs of the business considered. Location should be consistent with your purposes.

Product or Service: Is there a need for your product or service? If not apparent, can a demand for it be developed through advertising and provide a profitable return on the time and money you will be investing?

Bookkeeping: All transactions of your business must be accounted for to provide records for your own knowledge, as well as for reports required to meet reporting required by the government.

Records: Reports should be prepared for your own use. These should cover receivables, payables, inventory, payrolls, insurance, financial statements and periodic operating statements.

Management: This is the crucial element that either creates your success or expedites your failure. A study of and understanding of financial records and pertinent management experience will contribute to a successful operation.

Personnel: If your business goes beyond a one-man enterprise, sufficient, experienced staff must be available and trained properly to accommodate customers.

Inventory: Sufficient in quantity and quality to meet customer demand through all seasons.

Advertising: A necessary tool to help a business grow, using experienced personnel or an ad agency to select the most effective media with professionally-developed messages.

Free publicity: It's easier than you might think. Issue professionally-written news releases as appropriate, to national or regional media. Call up your local newspaper(s) radio and TV station(s) and suggest an interview.

Tax payments: Your government is a partner and an alert one. Make all payments accurately and on time, especially payments withheld from employees and held in trust by you.

Attorney: A reliable, business-experienced lawyer is needed to oversee the formation of proprietorship, partnership or corporation, to check leases and buy-and-sell agreements.

License and registration: You must be sure that the business you are considering is properly registered or licensed. Get a checklist from the local licensing bureau, chamber of commerce, or consult an attorney or accountant.

Outside assistance: Much outside help is available to you, most of it free, from government sources; from business organizations such as the local chamber of commerce; or from business development offices that might be located in capitols and major cities. Also check your library for books and journals that will help to guide and inform you.

The Executive Summary is a condensed outline of your entire business plan. Put it up front.

Accounting: Necessary But Not Necessarily Mysterious

Your business plan will of necessity be heavily laced with accounting figures. It is perhaps regrettable that so many entrepreneurs have a weakness for this extremely important ingredient and a business plan is, after all, the first step in organizing and funding a new business. Many accountants are quite competent to help you prepare a practical and acceptable business plan. This book, however, will take you a long way down the path of accounting proficiency. It might not teach you accounting, but it could provide you with sufficient inside knowledge to produce the kind of business plan that will serve as your guide, and as a creditable adjunct to a loan application. What is it then, that accounting pros could provide for you? What are bank loan officers and potential investors looking for in the plan you are about to produce for your business? Here are the critical elements.

Executive Summary

Put yourself into the place of a loan officer or investor who does not know you or your business idea. He gets dozens and even hundreds of proposals and applications each year. His time must be concentrated on those that are professionally prepared, complete and appear realistic. He wants to know, quickly, what it is all about. Your "Executive Summary" is a condensed outline – a "wrap-up" – of your entire business plan. Put it up front in one to two pages and answer the salient question the reviewer will have: "What's in it for me and how secure will my investment be?" Having answered all of that in brief fashion, append your Table of Contents and proceed to Step Two.

Your new business (most business plans are prepared for fledgling enterprises) probably does not have much of a creditable track record. As a substitute, offer an analysis of the market. Make thorough estimates, be critical, logical and probable. Don't just talk about your dreams, but about your expectations of realistic goals. Define your business in crystal-clear terms and state your goals and projections as honestly as you can at this point in time. What plan do you have to produce that better mousetrap, to have customers beat a path to your door, who will do each job and what his or her qualifications are, and how you expect to pay back the capital you expect to borrow.

Your financial projections should be tied to reality, to demonstrable industry figures. Lenders are usually pros in the money business, and they will spot unrealistic figures quickly.

Stick to your facts and do not malign the competition, but show your favored position in any competitive situation. Negativism has a way of coming back to haunt you, as many a politician has discovered.

There is much talk these days about 'innovative financing'—and indeed, there is no harm in being creative. Many lenders appreciate a pragmatic display of creativity, as long as it remains objective. Potential financial backers' first interest in their own interest.

Even if you prepare most of the business plan yourself, it will be well to include the actual services, or at least the names and references, of a professional accountant and attorney. The addition of professionals will assure that your plan is regarded as being soundly structured and will minimize unforeseen future liabilities.

While a business plan should be thorough, it should also be concise. A ponderous presentation could turn off an outsider. If you feel that corroborating evidence and appendices are necessary, put them in a separate addendum. The financier then will have the option to peruse the additional material.

If but one of the pieces of information in this book applies to you and your enterprise, then this book will have paid for itself. Even if a professional prepares a business plan for you and charges you thousands, you will have to supply the inside information. Be patient and study this book. It can not only save you money, but provide an invaluable learning process that can lead to one of the important and valuable tools of your new or expanding business.

Chapter I

Are You Ready for the Demands of Entrepreneurship?

- **Your Entrepreneurial Test**
- **A Banker's Viewpoint of Your Business Plan**
- **Twelve Components of a Business Plan**
- **Buying a Business**
- **Summation of the Executive Summary**

The Spirit of Entrepreneurship is an elusive characteristic. It appears to crop up more frequently among some people than others; among some ethnic groups more so than those who have rarely, if ever, been exposed to buying and selling, or the creative process, or working for oneself. It isn't all education and knowledge, though these certainly will help. Having the right upbringing such as a successful father or other family member "in the business" can be immeasurably useful, but this cannot be ordained or created.

In Figure 1 on the following page, we have showcased the POE Factor to try and explain the *Entrepreneurial Spirit*. POE stands for *Persistence, Optimism and Expertise*. Some people may learn the first two, but most cannot. You will develop expertise through diligent work and study. There are a few other, less-concrete ingredients, such as luck, opportunity, and a rich relative leaving you a large amount of money.

Luck borders on superstition. Opportunity, which often creeps silently into view, must be heard and seen to be realized. And depending on a financial windfall is worse than betting the slowest horse in a race to come in first. So where do we go from here?

No entrepreneur need feel lonely or in need of encouragement.

What Puts the $ into a $uccessful Entrepreneur?

The POE Factor. It stands for **Persistence, Optimism, Expertise.** Put the three together and you have the recipe for success. The steps to POE can include:

- Motivation to achieve and succeed, no matter how steep the road.

- Perpetual striving for quality in product and service, not necessarily perfection, but constant improvement.

- Veneration for the customer who is, after all, the the objective of all business planning.

- Long-term goals rather than quick-fix short-term gains.

- Dependence, despite a king-sized sense of individualism, on peers and peer groups who can boost the entrepreneur's well-being.

- Encouragement of entrepreneurial dreams that can lead to innovation and often, but not always, to profit-achievement.

The true entrepreneur rarely recognizes setbacks, but takes them as challenges to betterment, or simply to another road less traveled. Add to this potpourri a dollop of enthusiasm, plus an endless quest for knowledge, and the entrepreneur YOU will be an unbeatable economic force. Your Business Plan should express all of these ingredients. Like a cake in the oven, half-baked it will fall flat. Well prepared and executed, it is ambrosia that tinkles pleasantly in the till.

Remember: entrepreneurs average 3.8 failures before final success. A sound Business Plan, aided by persistence and knowledge, will enhance your chances for success. Like Armand Hammer, the oil tycoon, said *"When I work 14 hours a day, seven days a week, I get lucky."* It was his key to $uccess.

To find out whether *you* are ready to be an entrepreneur will take all of the above, and a little more. It takes good management and it takes money in that order.

Notice that when we named the two main ingredients of entrepreneurial success, we mentioned management first, and money second. Think about that for a moment.

There have been hundreds of good companies during the past years that were well financed, but eventually went bankrupt. Unlike federal governments that can borrow freely and print more money when needed, business people cannot practice deficit financing and survive. While money is always helpful and sometimes can even be a lifesaver, it is less important than a smart business leader who can plan and foresee problems before they occur, manage money astutely, and never accumulate more debts than assets.

Yes, money is important, but it takes backseat to management. That's where you may be armed with a few competitive advantages that another business operator may not have—Persistence, Optimism, Expertise. The POE Factor.

Persistence to keep on going when the going gets rough, and it invariably will, especially during the troublesome startup years. *Optimism* to know instinctively that there is always an alternative, that pitfalls are only holes in the road to be filled with opportunity. *Expertise* to be creative, innovative, reliable, quality-conscious, and forever seeking more knowledge to forge ahead.

And now we are ready if you are to see what makes you tick. Here is an Entrepreneurial Test that may give you a hint:

The Entrepreneurial Test

This is an examination of the most important ingredient in your business: *you*. It does not provide all the answers nor any magic solution, but it provides some guidelines, some parameters, that establish that *you* have a better-than-even chance for success in a business of your own. Nobody will judge the results of this test except *you*, for you are judge and jury of

When we named the two main ingredients of entrepreneurial success, we mentioned management first, and money second. Think about that.

your own fate. (Who said, "If it's to be, it's up to me"?) Your Entrepreneurial Test is a good exercise for you before you spend any money.

1. Being optimistic is one positive, even necessary trait, of the entrepreneur. Do you think you are? ___YES ___NO

2. The repetitiveness of industrial jobs can be boring. You, too, are easily bored by ordinary, rote tasks. In fact, you might even judge yourself to be a restless type of personality? ___YES ___NO

3. A child whose parent or parents were successful with their own business. Are you the progeny of parents who were successful with their own business? ___YES ___NO

4. You'd think that brilliant students would make the best entrepreneurs, but that hasn't been borne out by fact. Most entrepreneurs were only average students, and developed later. Were you? ___YES ___NO

5. Entrepreneurial personalities were usually self-contained youngsters— rarely members of athletic teams or tight groups. Were you always pretty self-sufficient? ___YES ___NO

6. Along similar lines, were you content as a youngster when you were alone? ___YES ___NO

7. When you were still in school, did you engage in any paid, entre-preneurial activities, such as babysitting, newspaper delivery, working part time, or helping run things at school? ___YES ___NO

8. Stubbornness as a child, or better said, determination, is a measurable trait. Do you think you were stubborn? ___YES ___NO

9. Did you handle any money as a youngster? Were you quite good at managing it?   ___YES   ___NO

10. Do you usually write down things? Make memos to yourself of tasks you have to do? Take good notes?   ___YES   ___NO

11. Entrepreneurs are calculated risk-takers and often venture into previously-uncharted areas. Do you think that you are that type?   ___YES   ___NO

12. Some take well-trod paths; others make paths for followers. Do you feel you are adventurous enough to venture into different directions?   ___YES   ___NO

13. Does getting stuck in a rut make you anxious, propel you into new areas and motivate you to think about going into new businesses or associations?   ___YES   ___NO

14. Put yourself in the seat of a loan officer at a financial institution. Would you regard an entrepreneur such as yourself as an acceptable risk?   ___YES   ___NO

15. Entrepreneurship takes determination and perseverance. Supposing your business went broke; would you start up again in a different direction?   ___YES   ___NO

16. Being in business is forgetting about the clock. Could you, or would you, devote the hours to being a successful entrepreneur that business independence often demands?   ___YES   ___NO

17. Are you the type who usually tackles or overlaps two or more projects at the same time? Finishes one task and begins another one right away?   ___YES   ___NO

18. While it is usually good to use the OPM (other people's money) method in business startups, would you risk your own savings to start up or expand a business of your own? ___YES ___NO

19. If you are willing to risk your own money, are you so convinced about the soundness of your business that you would ask others to risk their investment also? ___YES ___NO

20. Despite your entrepreneurial penchant and willingness to take calculated risks, would you rather research and market-test an idea first, or surge ahead and depend entirely on your gut feeling? You admit that you would act on the side of caution in this case, or would you? ___YES ___NO

OK, there it is. How did you make out? Frankly, how many times could you unequivocally and honestly say 'Yes'? If the overwhelming majority of answers were 'Yes,' go ahead. You will make a great entrepreneur. If not, better recheck your plans...

A Banker's Viewpoint of Your Business Plan

By this time you have hopefully been convinced that a business plan is a necessity if you want to start, operate and profit in a business of your own. It is doubly necessary if you have to rely on others to furnish you with capital.

There is no single way to prepare a business plan. Different business counselors, bankers, financial officers, accountants, lawyers and writers have various ideas as to the most effective method to make a presentation. So, with some humility, we present here a cross-section of what we feel is the most logical, acceptable and feasible way to create your business plan.

Look at your business plan as the constitution of your enterprise. Once it is completed, it will form the foundation, the platform, the basis of your business. Over the years, you may want to make additions and alterations to fit circumstances just like a constitution would receive.

Now look at the other side of the table. If you need startup and operating capital for your business, you will first of all search your own resources; then approach others, at banks or lending institutions, who are usually strangers to you. Here, then, sits that stranger. All he usually knows about you is what you have written down on those sheets of paper called your business plan. To him, you are a commodity from which he and his bank or institution intend to make a profit, and which will pay his salary. Got the picture? Now try to fill the frame.

Like a precious perfume, your business plan requires attractive packaging. The aromatic elixir is encased in a costly bottle, ensconced in a box and then wrapped in costly foil. Your business plan too, must be wrapped for attraction.

Many years ago when we first ventured out into the business world, an older friend gave us this bit of sage advice, which we have never forgotten. We'll pass it on to you, for what it's worth: *When applying for a job, always present yourself in good clothes.*

What all this preamble comes down to is this: If you think that your business plan is worth the paper it is written on, use the finest paper you can afford. Input your business plan into the computer and output it on the best stationery possible, neatly, professionally and flawlessly. Then encase it in a folder or spiral-bound clear plastic. Additionally, using a computer word processor or page-layout program makes it much easier and faster to make changes to both the content and the appearance of your plan. If you aren't skilled in using word processing software, a phone call to a computer users' group or a secretarial service should provide you with someone qualified to do it for you for a reasonable fee.

Complete your business plan. Use professional help, if you believe you need it especially in perfecting the financials. Be as thorough, as candid, as realistic as you can. You cannot fool yourself, and you certainly won't fool the professionals who examine your presentation and make the decision to lend many thousands of dollars to you, based on the premise and promise of your business plan.

Imagine the Founding Fathers of our country slaving over the document that we regard today as the blueprint of our nation. Your Business Plan is equally important to you.

23

Once your complete business plan is done, turn yourself into a critic. Make believe you are going to consider that business plan, but you certainly want to know what it contains. You have little time and perhaps less patience. There are 49,999 other business plans out there from which you could choose. So why should you risk your firm's funds on this one?

After your final polishing is done, have the plan checked by several others—including a qualified proofreader (or two). One additional word to the wise: Your business plan will project a much more polished and professional appearance if you prepare your plan with a good word processor.

By this time, we believe you can empathize with the financial officer who is going to peruse your business plan. So to make it more enticing, interesting and plausible your next step is to write an Executive Summary. It will be concise, exact, unadorned. It will be short and it is the key that will open the locked door to a loan.

Even though the Executive Summary is the first thing the prospective lender will read in your business plan, you are most likely to write it last. But remember, it is first impressions that last.

Twelve Components of a Business Plan:

1. Cover Letter

2. Business Identification

3. Business Purpose and Goals

4. Description of Business

5. Your Market Research

6. Competition

7. Management
   - Business Asset Management
   - Personnel Management

8. Location

9. Marketing Strategy

10. Financial Information

11. Keeping Records

12. Executive Summary

Buying a Business

The following section of the business plan is necessary only if you are acquiring somebody else's business, rather than starting your own. We need not be too concerned here with the philosophies behind such a move, but only with its impact on your business plan and your ability to borrow additional capital.

Buying somebody else's business is often a shortcut to profitable operations, since the business is already up and running. It's like refueling an airplane in midair or having it land to begin the takeoff procedure anew. With this advantage, however, come a few cautions:

- You might need more capital up front to take over somebody else's operating business;

- You need to know a great deal about the business you are acquiring; just because it is (hopefully) a well-run enterprise does not guarantee it will continue to be so, unless you truly understand it;

- You need to make sure that any inventory is clean, current, market valued and that employees and customers will remain loyal to you;

- You need to determine why the seller wants to sell his business if it is running so well.

An experienced accountant, lawyer, and banker on your side can be of immeasurable assistance, rather than relying on your gut feeling or even on the "advice" of the seller's broker.

Buying somebody else's business is often a shortcut to profitable operations.

Summation of the Executive Summary

When preparing your business plan for a loan application, it is customary to start out with an *Executive Summary* up front. The reason is that the loan officer is extremely busy. He or she wants to know immediately what your business is all about, how much money you want, how you plan to pay it back and what security you have to back the loan. Knowing this, you will prepare the entire business plan first; then extract the above four points from the body of the plan and put a synopsis of them up front in the "Executive Summary." It will be useful to make this summary as complete, concise and dramatic as possible. If your business revolves around a product, enclose a picture of the product. If it is a building or a business location, include a picture of that structure or plan of the location. If you have illustrative or explanatory literature, such as catalog sheets or brochures, attach them also. It's the old story: make your first impression a lasting one.

Here are the key elements of your summary

• Description of Your Business—what does it do; how long has it been in business; what is your management team like; why did you pick your particular location; what is your business's growth potential?

• Amount of Your Loan Request—what do you need the money for; for how long do you need it; how would you prefer the loan to be paid?

• Your Payback Plan—amount, number and timing of the payback; where will you get the money to repay the lender; what backup plan do you have in case your money for the payback does not come in as readily as you envision?

• Security for Your Loan—what is the true, current value of your collateral; how was this value appraised; how readily is it available in an emergency?

Chapter II

12 *Quick-and-Easy* Steps to Your Business Plan

Step 1: Introduction to the Business Plan

As you develop your thoughts, notes and figures for your Business Plan, determine first of all:

• How much you really need to borrow;

• How long will you need borrowed money;

• For how long a period you need it;

• Where you will get the money;

• A backup plan in case your present projection doesn't work out;

• What security will be offered as collateral;

• The current appraisal of your security and its availability.

There are three preliminary steps you need to take to start your actual Business Plan:

1.1 The Cover Letter

You need some good stationery on which to write this cover letter. The quality and design of your stationery is the first impression. Let it reflect your best effort, your quality, your image. The cost is minor when compared with the intended results.

It is said that *"You don't need to be a millionaire to dress like one."* Still, people judge you first by what they see on the outside. This is the way products are packaged. This is the way applicants, whether for loans or jobs, are regarded. This is one of the ways your business plan will be judged.

If your business plan is to be used as a presentation to a potential lender or financial institution, a cover letter, printed on good stationery, should introduce you and the purpose of your presentation. Here is an example:

****

Dear (name):

We are requesting your granting us a loan of $_____ for the purpose of _____. Repayment is anticipated over a period of _____. The source of repayment will be _____. We are offering you as collateral the items listed on the accompanying exhibit, complete with appraised valuation, having an approximate current value of $_____, conservatively stated.

We will greatly appreciate your serious consideration of this loan request, since this loan will be vital to the successful and profitable execution of our business plan, as enclosed. Should you require further information, please contact us at (phone number) _____.

Cordially,

(Signature[s])

Name(s)

Title(s)

Encl: Business Plan for _____

                                      (your company name)

****

1.2 Cover Sheet

Business Plan

for

(Your Company Name)

Prepared especially for

(Financial Officer's Name &

Lending Institution's Company Name)

1.3 Table of Contents

Step 2. Business Identification

This is the name you give your business, which then will appear on all of your stationery and anything that is imprinted with your business name—the outside sign(s), wrappings and cartons, vehicles and advertising. It is like the baptism of your business and very likely you will live with this name for the rest of your business life.

The real importance, in addition to identification, is to let your name tell your customers and clients who you are and what you do. It is important to give considerable attention to this vital function.

The business identification should not be the creation of a whim or something dashed off on the kitchen table over coffee. A good name will be appropriate to your business or profession, identify either you or your business function or location, and make a positive impact in the telephone directory, in your business signs, your business cards… wherever it may come to the attention of anyone who can influence your enterprise.

Your business letterhead and business cards should specify, if it isn't self-evident, precisely what your product or service is; your promotional materials (brochures & handout materials) and your advertisements should also detail how those products and/or services can benefit the reader (*i.e.*, your prospective customer). They should also include your phone and fax numbers, your business's E-mail address and (if applicable) and your Internet address. Be especially careful that each character in your E-mail and Internet addresses properly display each character in correct lower-case or upper-case, since these addresses are sometimes case-sensitive.

All of your business's printed materials should be professionally designed and present an attractive, consistent style; each of your printed materials should display your company logo and consistently adhere to your own established set of company-standard, easy-to-read typefaces.

If your business's purpose is self-evident, such as *"Smith's Auto Rentals,"* include your unique selling proposition such as *"Specializing in luxury cars,"* or *"Free and speedy 24-hour delivery and pickup."*

Business Identification Worksheet

1. The name of the business is

2. Business address

3. Actual location

4. Telephone

5. Tax or business registration number

6. Principals involved in business and contact address

7. Accountant of record and address and phone

8. Attorney of record and address and phone

9. Banker, location and phone

10. Insurance agent and address and phone

11. Other business consultant or advisor, address and phone

Step 3. Business Purpose

The purpose of your business might appear obvious to you when that bright idea first hits your mind. But will it still be pertinent a year down the road? Will the financial officer who examines your business plan be convinced that your purpose is realistic and destined for success?

This section of your business plan might require deeper thought than you first gave it. The old adage *"Sleep on it!"* might apply here. Of course, you have personal needs: making money and improving your lifestyle. These wealth-creating functions are obvious external reasons.

More reasons of your purpose are the sometimes subtle needs of our society: making a contribution to the endangered environment, improving the ethical conduct of your type of business, providing employment to your fellowman. If you spell out all these additional purposes of entrepreneurial creation, you will be more satisfied with yourself and with your business plan and so will your investors or lenders.

Will the financial officer be convinced your purpose is realistic?

Business Purpose (worksheet)

1. The goals of my proposed business are:

   _____

   _____

   _____

2. If an existing business, state purpose(s) of acquisition or expansion:

   _____

3. Your experience to enable you to successfully manage the above-described enterprise consists of:

   _____

   _____

4. How much money will be needed from:

   • Your own investment? . . . . . .$ _____

   • Other personal lenders? . . . . .$ _____

   • Loan from this institution? . .$ _____

5. How long will you make use of these funds? _____

6. How will these funds benefit the proposed business, in terms of:

   • Machinery or equipment _____

   • Inventory _____

   • Working capital _____

   • Other _____

7. Over what period of time do you intend to repay this loan? _____

8. Where will the funds for repayment come from?

   _____

   _____

9. Your collateral and market value _____ [$_____]

10. Who owns the collateral (described in #9)? _____

Step 4. Description of Business

It seems simple to say that your business does this and that, and that you are either a proprietorship, a partnership or a corporation. But there's more to it; in fact, there are a number of points that must be accounted for.

In 1624 (in his *Meditation 17*) English poet John Donne wrote *"No man is an island,"* an admonition that each of us and each of our endeavors is dependent upon and interdependent with other individuals and other institutions. Your enterprise itself will be functioning within the context of a larger society. Your choice of individuals and institutions with whom you will be associating can speak volumes about the viability of your enterprise, and can serve to determine the level of its success.

Many professionals and peers with whom you surround yourself and with whom you will do business will be helpmates, suppliers, and under-writers of your future success.

Your choices of banker, lawyer, accountant and insurance carrier, for example, indicate that you have planned carefully and thoroughly, and are planning to stay on this course for the long haul. If these advisors are recognized to be of sterling caliber, their implied association with you will enhance your status.

Equal advantages can come from your association with professional and trade societies, chambers of commerce, and leadership in professional, civic and academic organizations.

Description of Business (worksheet)

1. The legal description of the proposed business:

   _____

2. If corporation, where is it *or will it be* incorporated?_____

3. Other pertinent information: _____

4. Classification or government code of corporate business: _____

5. Is this a new business, expansion of your existing business, or purchase of an existing business? _____

6. When are you projecting to begin operation?_____

7. If this is an existing business, outline its history:

   _____

   _____

   _____

8. Your projected operating schedule of business:

   _____

9. Is this a: Seasonal business? _____ Year-round business? _____

10. Describe your plans for managing the business, including personnel, stock and inventory:

    _____

    _____

    _____

11. Who are your outside vendors and what will they be providing?
    • vendor: _____ supplying:_____
    • vendor: _____ supplying:_____
    • vendor: _____ supplying:_____
    • vendor: _____ supplying:_____

12. Terms of supply acquisition or credit available:

_____

13. What specific prices and discounts have been quoted by the suppliers for the above-mentioned products?

_____

_____

_____

14. What (if any) technical or management assistance will suppliers render?_____

_____

15. Who are your outside contractors and what will they be providing?
   • contractor: _____ providing:_____
   • contractor: _____ providing:_____
   • contractor: _____ providing:_____
   • contractor: _____ providing:_____
   • contractor: _____ providing:_____

   Their terms? _____

16. If you are planning to construct a building, supply all specifics, costs, titles: _____

_____

17. Why will this business be successful and profitable? _____

_____

18. Who started the business you are buying and when? _____

19. What do you think are the real reasons that this business is for sale?

_____

Step 5. Market Research

YOUR MARKET RESEARCH—
Pre-Business Plan Planning

If you are planning to build a better mousetrap, make sure that there are mice out there. While this might sound like a simplistic statement, it will surely come as no surprise that many businesses lose or even go bankrupt because there were no mice to catch in their "better mousetrap."

The answer, of course, is to do your planning before you make a marketing decision, and especially before you spend any money. All too often, one major factor, typical among entrepreneurs, gets in the way of this simple logic: *enthusiasm for the new idea and the conviction that the world is waiting to beat a path to your door.* Sometimes it is; most often it isn't.

This pre-planning is called Market Research. It sounds like a very ponderous, costly and time-consuming process—and it can be. However there are some shortcuts that can be taken. Suffice to say, doing market research now is a lot less time and energy consuming, and certainly a great deal more cost-effective, than doing it later and possibly failing.

Market research is called for; complete, in-depth investigation that will provide you with pragmatic and rational answers. Limited and falsely directed research will only lead to wrong conclusions.

It is unlikely that an enthusiastic entrepreneur will hesitate for too long on the side of apathy and inertia. This, too, can be deadly. As Breen and Blankenship point out in their very useful book, "Do-It-Yourself Market Research," *"It is too easy to say 'no' to a new product or a new idea. An action that is never taken cannot fail. It might have been profitable, but no one will ever know."*

Steven Harper in his book, "Starting Your Own Business," compared the market to a horse, and you, the entrepreneur, as the rider. As he put it, *"No jockey ever carried his horse across the finish line."* In other words, the market must be there to support your product or service. If there is any doubt in your mind that the need exists, or that you have the skill and means to create a market niche, you'd better go over your plan again.

> **The best-built mousetrap will not attract customers unless there is a clearly-defined path on which potential buyers can approach.**

With all the caveats that we dredge up to make you more cautious about potential risks, intuition, imagination and ideas still play a big role. Even market research cannot always substitute for the innate tools of the entrepreneur. However, market research can fill in the gaps that intuition cannot account for.

Take one example: Saturation Statistics. These figures from the U.S. Census Bureau's *Retail Trade Charts* tells how many people it takes to enable a business to survive and prosper. Here are average numbers:

- Hardware Store—requires at least 8,000 people within the immediate market

- Barber shop—2,200

- Florist shop—8,600

- Nursery and garden supplies—26,000

- Restaurant—8,500

- Ladies' fashion store—5,000

- Furniture store—3,000

- Bookstore—26,000

- Stationery store—60,000

One caution: the above figures are conservative and depend upon your ambition. They also refer to existing population, not potential customers. In a new area or a new shopping center, your research must take into consideration potential development, future competition in reaction to population growth, and even the type of competition—franchise, highly promotional businesses, anticipated road pattern changes, proximity of customer centers that exist or are projected, and other factors.

The more meaningful figures that you have at your disposal, the easier it will be to prepare a business plan that will work for you—and open the doors to potential loan demands.

FIVE TYPES OF MARKETING RESEARCH YOU CAN DO

1. Market Research: Finding out the real needs and wants of potential buyers, determining the specific market segment, assessing the market area, evaluating competition, spotting trends heretofore obscured.

2. Promotion Research: Determining the best strategy to reach your market, evaluating media, comparing costs and results.

3. Product Research: Ascertaining the public's receptivity, assuring pricing in the marketplace and in relation to competition, determining quality of product in actual use, checking distribution, naming, and packaging methods.

4. Sales Research: Evaluating performance, training and compensation of internal and external sales personnel, empathy with product, service follow-up, assigned territories or job station.

5. Company Research: Checking overall trends in your business, assessing company image, adequacy of location, morale, quality control, company ethics, adherence to environmental concerns and government regulations.

Methods of marketing research can include surveys (personal interviews, telephone calls or mail questionnaires), observation (observing customer behavior by eye contact or electronic equipment), and/or experimental methods (actually establishing test situations in a store, trade show booth, display, or test advertisements). Because products and services needs and consumers are constantly changing, marketing research should be a continuing part of your business operation.

Step 6. Competition

Competition will invariably exist. If you think you have an exclusive niche in your market, take advantage of it as much as possible. The chances are, however, that you will have plenty of competition who will compete, directly or indirectly, for the same market as you do. You can learn a great

So if you want to learn quickly, see what your competitors have done right and what they have done wrong.

deal from a larger and older competitor. Many of these have proven themselves as vulnerable to time and change as other enterprises, and many famed companies have disappeared from view—usually more because of faulty management than lack of financing—it was invariably competition that did them in. Somebody built a better company.

So if you want to learn quickly, see what your competitors have done right and what they have done wrong. Sometimes you can learn a lot from a non-competitor in the same business, one who happens to be located in another market or in another city. Such a study can be more valuable than hiring a costly consultant—and it looks ever so good in your business plan.

Competition Worksheet

1. Names and locations of your nearest competitors:

_____

2. Do you have any realistic information on their status? Proof?

_____

3. In what ways will you be competitive (or better)? _____

_____

4. How will you be different? Be specific about your advantages and how you can meet and beat competition, if needed.

_____

_____

_____

5. What is your estimate of the competition's market share?

_____

6. What strategies can you generate to obtain some of that market share? Over what time period? At what cost?

_____

_____

Step 7. Management

Management is perhaps the very first and foremost consideration in any business. The person or persons who run the business will determine, more than any of the other factors, whether the enterprise has a chance to succeed or is doomed to crash with the first ill wind. While a single proprietorship is easy to describe, providing you are completely candid with yourself, a multiple-management business is fraught with complications.

Other members of the management team need to be analyzed closely and with complete frankness. Partners, especially, will come under scrutiny, as will specialized executives who are slated to perform functions that you cannot do. Such dependency makes you vulnerable and all possibilities must be taken into account when creating a workable and pragmatic business plan.

We cannot emphasize enough that management is the Number One reason businesses succeed or fail. Money is important, of course, and in the minds of many startup entrepreneurs, money is the first consideration. But experienced business people, and certainly financial officers, know that the "You Factor" determines whether an enterprise will likely grow or crash.

The determination of this step is difficult also for emotional reasons. As an entrepreneur you are ready, willing and able. It is indeed difficult to admit that you have shortcomings. But it's your life and your money. If you need more counsel, more training, more knowledge, get it now before you spend your hard-earned money and time.

We cannot emphasize enough that management is the Number One reason businesses succeed or fail.

Management Worksheet

1. Attach a detailed resumé of each principal in the business.

2. Name each principal and related business experience in reference to the new business: _____

   _____

3. What are job descriptions of each of the above? Salaries? Costs of benefits? _____

   _____

   _____

   _____

4. What external management assistance can you call on, if and when necessary? _____

   _____

   _____

   _____

7.1 Personnel

Personnel is also a weighty decision that must be accounted for in the business plan. At the beginning of many small enterprises, the owner and his family do double-duty or, at best, arrangements can be made to utilize part-time personnel who work usually less than 20 hours a week, or on a basis other than a firm salary or hourly rate.

For purposes of your planning, this determination must be made as accurately as possible, since it impacts your cash needs. Personnel compensation must usually be made immediately and usually before income is derived from their contributions. The fiscal officer who might examine your business plan is especially interested in your commitments to hired personnel and its long-range implications on your cash flow. Remember, too, that it is wise to establish in writing a clearly-understood employee policy.

Personnel Worksheet

1. Will you need to hire any people? If so, what are the job titles, functions and expected salaries? _____

    _____

    _____

    _____

2. What training and additional benefits must you provide?_____

    _____

    _____

    _____

3. Can your business employ part-time employees? _____

    _____

    _____

    _____

4. Are any of the proposed employees your family members? _____

    _____

    _____

    _____

5. Briefly detail a succession policy, in the event you become incapable of managing the business yourself: _____

    _____

    _____

    _____

    _____

    _____

    _____

Step 8. Business Location

Location will be of primary interest to your interviewer at the bank or lending institution. Business experts have learned there are three factors that will affect the health of your retail business: location, location, location.

In other sections of this book we have mentioned some of the criteria that need to be weighed in choosing a location for your business and the pitfalls that need to be regarded before signing any lease obligation. This section in your business plan needs to be completed carefully, both for your own protection and guidance, and for the examining lending officer. He knows, as you should, that a misstep in this section can cost you your business and obligate you for many years to come.

If your business is operating out of your home—and a growing number of small startups and "second time around" businesses are home-based—you need to make sure that the space is adequate to your needs, relatively free of family interference and temptations, and is zoned appropriately. There are tax advantages that may be considered, too.

If you sign a lease for external premises, do some quick arithmetic for your own information and for your business plan:

1000 sq. ft. office @ $12 sq. ft. for 3 years = $36,000

2000 sq. ft. retail store @ $10 sq. ft. for 5 years = $100,000

5000 sq. ft. warehouse @ $5 sq. ft. for 2 years = $50,000

Add to these costs such "peripheral expenditures" as utilities, shared maintenance costs, refuse removal, improvements, *et al.*

Retail business experts have learned that there are three factors that determine the success of your retail business: location, location, location.

Location Worksheet

1. State your reason(s) for choosing the location you've selected:

   _____

   _____

2. Is the neighborhood appropriate for your business? _____

3. What are the zoning restrictions? _____

4. Other area businesses? Any competitive? _____

5. Why is this location your first choice? _____

   _____

6. What other locations have you explored? _____

   _____

7. What is the rental or purchase cost? _____

8. Is this location permanent? If not, when will it change? _____

9. Do you own or lease the building you are in? _____

10. Describe the lease terms, taxes, future increases clause: _____

    _____

    _____

    _____

11. Enclose a floor plan of the facility.

12. If you need to make alterations or renovations, attach revised floor
    plans and cost estimates. Will the landlord pay all or part of these
    leasehold improvements?

Location Evaluations of Different Sites

The following worksheet can help you to decide which prospective locations would be best for your business planning. Use a rating of 1-to-5 in ascending order with 5 being the most favorable. All factors may not be relevant for all types of businesses, so disregard those not relevant to your business, and divide your total score by the number of applicable questions x five. For example, if 17 of the questions are applicable to your business, your maximum *possible* count is 17 x 5, or 85. If your total count is 78, then 78 ÷ 85 = 92%.

LOCATION .... Worse ⟵⟶ Better

FACTOR	1	2	3	4	5
Busy shopping area	___	___	___	___	___
Street access to premises	___	___	___	___	___
Traffic flow	___	___	___	___	___
Pedestrian traffic	___	___	___	___	___
Parking facilities	___	___	___	___	___
Public transportation	___	___	___	___	___
Street location	___	___	___	___	___
Nearest competition	___	___	___	___	___
Display area	___	___	___	___	___
Ease of entry and exit	___	___	___	___	___
Rear access for deliveries	___	___	___	___	___
Required utilities	___	___	___	___	___
Building condition	___	___	___	___	___

Required improvements	___	___	___	___	___
Cost of rent	___	___	___	___	___
Length of lease	___	___	___	___	___
Location vacancy rate	___	___	___	___	___
History of site	___	___	___	___	___
Property taxes	___	___	___	___	___
Suitable zoning	___	___	___	___	___

Total count: _____ (divide this number by your maximum possible count to determine your score; the closer to 100%, the better your location).

Step 9. Marketing Strategy

Marketing is the strategic plan to put you in touch with the customer in order to satisfy their NEEDS, WANTS or DESIRES. This should be based on your market research and plays a vital role in successful business ventures. The key element of a successful marketing plan is to know your customers—their likes, dislikes, and expectations. By identifying these factors, you can develop a marketing strategy that will allow you to arouse and fulfill their needs.

You must understand your customer before you can develop or offer a product or service that they will want to buy.

If you are introducing an innovative or new product, you must try to create a desire for the product, but this will take a great deal of marketing effort in the areas of advertising, publicity, sales promotion, and public relations. Novelty products, such as pet rocks, have a shorter life than products that will fill a need.

COMPETITION

Competition is a way of life: your business's competition exists now or will develop soon. Nations compete in the global marketplace, as do domestic entrepreneurs in their local spheres of interest.

IBM is an example of intense competition in the personal computer field. A newspaper report stated *"IBM, struggling again to salvage its fortunes as the world's premier computer company, announced sharp cutbacks in jobs and production lines and said it would probably lay off workers for the first time in its 78-year history."* The past few years have seen this reduction in work forces with many large firms worldwide.

Start a file on each of your competitors' advertising and promotional materials and their pricing strategy techniques. Review these files periodically, to monitor when and how often they advertise, sponsor promotions and offer sales. Use this information to determine your marketing strategy.

PRICING AND SALES

Pricing strategy is another marketing technique you can use to improve your overall competitiveness. It is a good idea to get a feel for the pricing strategy that your competitors are using. Do not let your competitors determine your pricing. Remember that price is only one part of the overall image—the service you provide your customers is equally or more important. Some of the pricing strategies you may consider are:

1. Direct product or service cost + operating expenses + desired profit

2. Be in a competitive position

3. Pricing below or above competition

4. Multiple pricing for quantities or different levels

The key to success is to have a well-planned strategy, to establish your policies, constantly monitor inventory turns, prices and operating costs to ensure profits. Keep abreast of the changes in the marketplace, because these changes will affect your competitiveness and profit margins.

ADVERTISING AND PUBLIC RELATIONS

You must not forget that money you borrow must be paid back; this money must be earned out of the proceeds of your business.

The purpose of advertising and publicity functions is to help move goods and services. Virtually every successful enterprise incorporates a measured investment of their marketing budget into these functions.

For your own reference, 2 to 5 percent of sales revenue for advertising might be appropriate based on your retail location, customer traffic, sales distribution, type of manufacturing image required, or service. Maintain a projected advertising/publicity calendar to control your budget and expenditure results. Continuously monitor and analyze *promotion costs versus results* directly traceable to these efforts.

If you are applying for outside financing, your business plan needs to account for and detail your advertising investment. We prefer to call this line item an investment rather than an expenditure. The reason is purely psychological. Good advertising should return a profit on your investment.

Publicity is virtually cost-free, although publicity results may be unpredictable. It is also very much underused and misunderstood. If you are not familiar with publicity techniques, then discuss your situation with a professional or read a good book on the subject.

Your Marketing Strategy Worksheet

1. WHO are your customers? DEFINE your target market(s):

_____

_____

2. WILL your markets continue growing? Remain steady? Decline?

_____

_____

3. WILL your markets be large enough to expand; are there restrictions?

_____

_____

4. HOW will you attract, hold, increase your market share?

_____

_____

5. WHAT will be your strategy to promote sales?

_____

_____

6. WHAT will be your pricing strategy?

_____

_____

7. WHAT will you do better than your competitors?

_____

_____

8. WHAT customer services will you offer?

_____

_____

9. WHICH benefits of your product line will you promote?

_____

_____

10. WHY will customers buy from you?

_____

_____

Step 10. Financial Information

This is the make-or-break section. It is the one a potential lender will understand best and will examine most closely for completeness, accuracy and realism. Even if you do not require outside capital, it is vital that you determine all of these figures accurately and realistically. It is sometimes better to err on the side of conservatism, than to be overly optimistic and be caught with your bank balance in the red.

It would be wise, too, to look over some of the pitfalls mentioned elsewhere in this book. Uneducated predictions are of little use, but experience and networking can be immensely useful.

Economic circumstances beyond your control, catastrophes of nature, sudden obsolescence caused by shifting customer preferences, zoning and road pattern changes, recessions that affect sales and collections all demand that you factor in a good percentage for "unforeseens."

Financial Information includes six sections, plus a seventh one in case you are buying someone else's business, which requires special information.

10.1 Capital Requirements

Every business needs some capital. Even if you have zero expenses (for example, if you are a consultant working out of your home, you have to account for one major expense: your own living costs, especially until such time that your business can generate sufficient income to meet your personal expenses. However, bear in mind that:

• your own assets might provide you with sufficient working capital or your family could pool its fiscal resources

• friends who share your entrepreneurial enthusiasm may want to get in on your business

• you might not need as much capital as you had thought

• you can lease or rent equipment rather than buying it outright

- you can hire part-time or per-job personnel rather than assuming a burdensome payroll

- you might consider a monied partner to put up capital and share in potential profits

- you could look into various methods of non-traditional, innovative funding such as a grant, an incubator (cooperative) association or supplier financing ("strategic alliances")

- you must not forget that money you borrow must be paid back, normally with interest, and that this money must be earned out of the proceeds of your business.

Should you still go out to a traditional money source, and you have carefully weighed all of the above nine considerations, match your capital requirement loan request with your current, negotiable collateral and start.

10.2 Depreciable Assets

In your business you have something of worth. It can be a building and the land on which it stands. It can be rolling stock, such as cars and trucks. It can be machinery used in an office or in production and warehousing. Or it could be inventory of merchandise destined for resale.

Most of these assets depreciate over a period of time, although some fixed assets, like real estate, could go up in value. The tax authorities may be most interested in your depreciable assets and they have fairly firm regulations about taking value reductions on them.

Most assets reduce in value due to obsolescence, wear and tear, accidental damage, and changes in consumer preferences. Such reductions in asset value are bookkeeping entries and do not represent any hard cash outlays. No funds need to be earmarked for such depreciation, though if such assets are pledged as collateral, depreciation might have to be supplemented with cash infusion in order to maintain your collateral's value.

In assessing value of real estate and land, the improvements upon the land and the land itself must be determined separately. For accounting purposes, two types of depreciation are used:

Straight Line Depreciation which is based on the estimated life of the item for bookkeeping purposes. Buildings might depreciate in 20 years, giving you a depreciation of five percent annually. A piece of machinery or truck might have a five-year depreciation, which allows you to reduce its value by 20 percent each year. Your country's tax guidelines need to be consulted annually.

Declining Balance Method of Depreciation is used when even quicker recovery of your investment is desirable. The tax authority may limit depreciation of the straight-line method. Example: If you choose to depreciate a truck costing $20,000 in two years instead of five years, you could take a $10,000 depreciation instead of the normal $4,000 depreciation. However, it is always prudent to consult an authority such as your accountant, on what is safe and acceptable for the particular year in question.

10.3 Pro Forma Balance Sheet

[Note: The term "Pro Forma" refers to the fact that the item (in this case the balance sheet) is projected, or before-the-fact, rather than actual, which would necessarily be after-the-fact. This form displays the Assets, Liabilities and Equity of the business, which serves to indicate how much investment will be required by the business and how much of it will be used as Working Capital in its operation.]

10.4 Break-Even Analysis

An examination of the activity when your total revenue equals your expenses. This juncture is called the break-even point. You need to determine, realistically, when your business activity reaches that point and then plan to go beyond it in order to make a profit. You can determine the break-even point either in currency or in units of merchandise. You may either, let's say, do a gross volume of $100,000 in order to equal your expenses, or you can sell 10,000 items at $10 apiece, equaling your $100,000 break-even point.

10.5 Projected Income Statement

The profit-and-loss statement for a specific length of time, usually monthly, if you're starting a new business, or for three years ahead if you have an established business. If you do not have specific and reasonably accurate figures based on your experience or past performance, then trade, industry or government figures can be consulted and adjusted for local conditions. At best, such a projection is reasonably accurate, rarely totally so. Its foundation is a number of educated guesses, but the more educated, the more accurate they will be. As we've said before, if you do err, let it be on the conservative side. Being overly optimistic could leave you with problems.

10.6 Cash Flow Projection and Analysis

Cash flow is the actual net income of a business. You cannot count money that is owed to you, because that money is only on your books, not in your pocket. However, for bookkeeping purposes, many businesses, especially corporations, will count depreciation, depletion, amortization and charges to reserves.

To be on the safe side, follow the old motto, *"Don't count your chickens 'til they're hatched."* Too many small businesses have troubles because they counted money that was coming in, supposedly, by the end of the month. When it did not, because customers were late, negligent, had troubles of their own, or other priorities, cash flow was diminished to dangerously low levels. In such cases, businesspeople had to resort to high-interest temporary loans, or had to factor their receivables by 70 to 80 percent.

Distorting cash flow figures can only hurt you. It will never fool the banker or lender. Your analysis needs to be ultra conservative, simply because it is in your own interest, even if you do not plan to borrow additional money.

Financial Information Checklist

> *Your analysis needs to be ultra conservative, simply because it is in your own interest, even if you do not plan to borrow additional money.*

___ 1. Balance sheet for the past three years if an established business; current balance sheet if this is a new business

___ 2. Operating statement same as (1)

___ 3. Project cash flow for three years (*month-by-month* if you're starting a new business; *quarterly* if you have an established business)

___ 4. Breakdown analysis same as (3)

___ 5. Financial statement for each principal, co-signor and/or guarantor of the business

___ 6. Personal or business tax returns for the three past years

___ 7. Capital equipment: if you need any, attach list of items, estimated cost or value of each

___ 8. Appraisal form from a bank-approved appraiser showing existence and current value of any real estate, vehicles, equipment and/or machinery owned by the business

___ 9. Assets that are owned or may be owned in the near future that should be disclosed.

Financial Information Worksheet
for Buying an Existing Business

1. Who determined the acquisition price? How much is it?

   _____

   _____

2. How much will you pay for "goodwill" (this is the established-customer
   base that comes with the business, which is referred to as "goodwill"
   in some countries)? _____

   _____

   _____

3. Will the seller take back any portion of the purchase price as a loan?
   On what terms? _____

   _____

   _____

4. Attach lists of visible assets, creditors and their terms, value and age of
   inventory, capital assets, any liabilities for which you will be
   responsible, appraisers' confirmations, photographs of building
   and/or location.

Step 11. Keeping Records

Records must be archived for some period of time, usually ranging from one to seven years. Full instructions may be obtained from the tax authority or your accountant. For the purposes of running a business adequately, accurately and efficiently, the following records must be considered and accounted for in your business plan:

• Day-by-day sales with weekly, monthly, quarterly and annual summaries

• *Perpetual inventory* to determine both availability and value of goods at hand, and re-ordering scheduling *(the term "perpetual inventory" refers to the maintenance of continuously-updated sales and inventory records, often with the implementation of computer barcode pricing and computerized reporting and reordering systems).*

• Sales taxes

• Cash sales

• Credit sales

• Customer records (names, addresses, sales, payments, purchase patterns)

• Sales promotions and results

    - Detailed expenses, including:

    - Personnel costs—including taxes, withholdings, *et al.*

    - Equipment acquisitions through purchase or lease, including vehicles

    - Leases and lease terms/conditions

    - Loans and repayment schedules

In a projected or new business, many of the above figures will be estimates. For an established business these should be actual up-to-date amounts. If you plan to purchase an existing business, records should be provided to you for your analysis and your accountant's and/or attorney's study. Record-keeping requires discipline and timeliness. ***The need will not go away; delay only makes record-keeping more difficult and less accurate.***

Step 12. Executive Summary

We have left this part for last, although you'll put *The Executive Summary* up front in your business plan.

Here is why your *Executive Summary* goes up front:

Your *Executive Summary* is an overall view of your business. It includes what you plan to do with it, what its potential is, how much money you need and how much money the business will generate. It reveals the return on investment (ROI) and how and when the investor (including the entrepreneur) can expect to get his money back.

The importance of your *Executive Summary* cannot be overstated. Financial investors and bank loan officers will often skim through the business plan, reading only those parts that are of interest to them. However, these experts *always* read your *Executive Summary*. Thus it's vital that you present the essence of your business plan in this *Summary*.

Your *Executive Summary* should include:

1. Specifically what you plan to achieve with your business

2. Objectives you intend to reach

3. How you intend to reach these objectives

4. Who will be responsible for meeting these objectives

5. What capitalization will be required to achieve them, including how such money, if borrowed, can be earned and repaid

These five short paragraphs should occupy less than one page; if you make them complete and dramatic enough, they will open doors for you.

That, in brief, is your *Executive Summary* and the outline of your business plan.

> **The importance of your Executive Summary cannot be overstated.**

Appendix

There are at least a dozen other considerations that could go into a business plan or matters that might be asked during a loan application process. They are listed here though you might have more.

Two reasons for providing as complete a series of documents as possible for the Plan are (1) so you will know exactly where you stand, and (2) so the financial officer to whom you may want to apply for a loan knows he is dealing with a professional.

Miscellaneous Checklist

1. If your business is a franchise, enclose the Franchise Agreement and disclosure statement

2. All pertinent contracts including lease

3. All business agreements

4. Management contracts

5. Maintenance agreements

6. Roster of major customers, annual purchases, terms

7. List of principal suppliers, annual volume, line of credit, terms

8. Credit card and credit system you use

9. Publicity that might have been generated

10. Annual report

11. Name of insurance carrier

12. Patents or copyrights owned

13. Other pertinent legal documents

You have now become acquainted with the various ingredients you'll use to create your business plan. It's time now for you to actually create one.

Let's continue...

Chapter III

Sample Business Plan: Retail Store

Your business plan should be "packaged" like a precious piece of jewelry or expensive perfume. In selling there is a saying: "When you want to make a good impression, put your best foot forward, and have your shoes well-shined."

The way you present the business plan can make a favorable first impression. That means: have a good cover on it. Use good stationery and double check it for errors.

Most bankers and financial officers prefer a summary up front, rather than at the end. In this way they can tell immediately, without wasting their valuable time, whether they are interested in your proposition or not. This summary is not as easy to write as it might seem. Sometimes it is more difficult to say in a hundred or two hundred words what you might more easily say in one thousand.

The worked-out example of a business plan, which follows this outline, is about a typical retail store. Follow this outline step-by-step and you will be assured correct results for your own needs as well as for presentation to a potential lender.

When you want to make a good impression, put your best foot forward, and have your shoes well-shined.

The 12 Steps

Step 1. Introduction to the Business Plan
Cover Letter
Cover Sheet for Business Plan
Table of Contents

Step 2. Business Identification

Step 3. Purpose
Statement of Purpose: why are you presenting this business plan

Step 4. Description of Business

Step 5. Market Research: Pinpointing Your Customer

Step 6. Competition: How Good are They?

Step 7. Management: Establishing credibility and establishing goals;
Personnel

Step 8. Business Site: Location, Location, Location

Step 9. Marketing Strategy

Step 10. Financial Information: Capital Requirement; Equipment;
Balance Sheet; Break-Even Analysis; Projected Income
Statement; Profit and Loss; Cash Flow Projection and Analysis

Step 11. Keeping Records: 3 years of personal history, business history
and tax records

Step 12. Executive Summary: one page synopsis
(to be placed after Step 3 once you have completed it and your
plan is assembled for submittal.)

Miscellaneous Checklist

Appendix:

- Copy of lease

- Contract, if business is purchased

- Franchise Agreement, if it's a franchise

- Partnership Agreement, if it's a partnership

- Articles of Incorporation, if it's a corporation

- Plan of location or property layout

- Agent Agreement, if one or more are engaged

- Client Contracts, if such commitments exist

Sample Business Plan: Retail Store

There are millions of retail stores in the world. Many of them sell some form of women's clothes. We have chosen one particular store as an example for our business plan. It is an imaginary store, but typical of one owned and operated by a middle-aged person who has accumulated long, in-depth experience in women's clothes, is self-sufficient economically, has accumulated fairly substantial cash reserves and equity, and has now arrived at a stage in life when he wants to become an entrepreneur independent of bosses and others' wiles and whims.

Our "sample" store will be a startup; that is, it will be a brand-new store, not a franchise or a store bought from a previous owner. This situation, too, is the most typical scenario, although more and more entrepreneurs are choosing the other two popular routes: buying an existing store or opening a franchise business. The reason for the latter trend: it is a short-cut to achieving a measurable stride of business volume and has a greater potential of survival and success. It also takes more up-front cash.

Your own Business Plan can be based upon this sample plan.

Our sample will stock and sell ladies' coats, raincoats, jackets, accessories. It might add additional related lines in the future, but initially, these are the principal clothing items for sale. They are ones the owner knows best from his prior experience; these are the items he feels will sell best and are the most-competition-proof at this time.

Your own business plan, whether for a startup, an established, or an expanding business, or whether planned as a tool for a business loan application, can be based upon this sample plan. Of course you might inject different elements to custom-tailor your own business plan to your particular situation. But this plan presents all the basic elements for a retail store of any type, as well as for most businesses.

Remember then: this sample business plan is only a guide to creating your own personal business plan; it is accurate only as an example of how to prepare your own business plan. The contents, figures, names, projections and entries are not authentic. You need to gather your own information for your business and corroborate it with appropriate market research.

Step 1 Introduction to the Business Plan

1.1 Suggested Cover Letter

Your Letterhead
Date
Name of Your Financial Officer
Name of Your Bank
Address
City

Dear _____:

Thank you for seeing me last _____ and discussing my plans to start a retail business in _____.

Enclosed is our business plan for *Worthmore's Fashions*. This confidential report is presented to you for your consideration of a $40,000 SBA-guaranteed loan.

The above loan is to be repaid monthly over a seven (7) year period, plus interest.

I will call you within a week for a follow-up appointment to discuss mutually-acceptable terms with you.

The proposed loan will be used for working capital, to back up my own investment of at least $60,000. You will note in my financials that our projected startup costs, including new inventory, amounts to $60,825.

As a long-time client of your bank, I am sure you will give your personal consideration to this loan proposal.

Sincerely yours,

Mary Worthmore dba *Worthmore's Fashions*

1.2 Cover Sheet

Name and Address of Business

Name, Address and Phone Number

of the Preparer of This Document

Business Plan

Mary Worthmore d/b/a

Worthmore's Fashions

1000 Main Street

Prosperity, PA 15329

Submitted by:

Mary Worthmore

(814) 555-1234

January 20, 2002

Step 1.3

TABLE OF CONTENTS

This is optional, but desirable if the business plan is lengthy or if the enclosures (appendix) are numerous.

TABLE OF CONTENTS

Introduction

Statement of Purpose

Need in Community

Appropriateness of Location

Experience of Management

Equity Production

Executive Summary

Description of Business

Products

Primary Suppliers

Customer Services

Market Research

Target Market

Competition

Strategy vs Competition

Management

Personnel

Location

Legal Structure

Tax Returns, past three years

Lease Agreement

Store Floor Plan

Leasehold Improvement Agreement (if separate from Lease)

Fixture Purchase Quotations

Office Equipment Lease Agreement

Insurance Schedule and Quotations

Service Agreements: Accountant, Lawyer

Prime Suppliers' Correspondent, if pertinent

Demographics

Automobile Lease or Installment Purchase, if any

Mortgage Statement, if any

Advertising Contracts, if any already signed

Copies of Certificates, Diplomas, Honors

Step 2 Business Identification

Worthmore's Fashions

1000 Main Street

Prosperity, PA 15329

(814) 555-1234

Tax ID# 525-70-5874

**Principals
Mary Worthmore
1000 Main Street
Prosperity, PA 15329
(814) 673-1424**

Accountant
Albert Able
(814) 555-8910

Attorney
Philip Peterson
(814) 555-4567

Banker
George Given
(814) 555-1112

Insurance
Ms. P.R. Otect
(814) 555-1314

Consultants
A.D. Vice
(814) 555-1516
Paul Wiseman
(814) 555-1718

Why are you preparing this Business Plan for someone else's eyes and requirements?

Step 3 Business Purpose

3.1 Statement of Purpose

This business plan is prepared (1) as a guide for management and (2) as supportive evidence that a business loan will be useful for the rapid growth of the business and can be repaid promptly out of projected cash flow.

Need in Community

The growth of Prosperity, based on state, municipal and Chamber of Commerce statistics, and the rise of a well-paid business and professional class of women shoppers, assures the concomitant growth of *Worthmore's Fashions*. With very limited competition in the market for the merchandise proposed, this store is needed to round out the demand of the foregoing buying group. Advance marketing studies and examining of traffic in markets ten or more miles away, which now are magnets for local shoppers, indicate that *Worthmore's Fashions* can help to round out market needs within the area and keep much business "at home."

Appropriateness of Location

The leased property at 1000 Main Street is a high-traffic corner near convenient parking and an estimated customer base of at least 10,000 working women. The lease is a reasonable one and offers renewal options well into the future.

Experience of Management

The sole proprietor of *Worthmore's Fashions* has had 20 years of experience in all facets of the women's fashion trade and store/department management. This is detailed in the section on Management.

Equity Production

Because of the need for this type of store, a growing customer base, and the experience of management, our projections indicate rapid equity production within a few months. Personal investment of owner is in excess of outside capitalization, assuring also that equity production will be of prime concern. Subsequent financials indicate that ample payback opportunity is assured by a healthy cash flow.

Executive Summary

You compiled (in Step 12) your synopsis of what your business plan is all about. Restate your outline here in order to provide your lender with a quick and clear overview of your proposal.

Executive Summary

A significant market opportunity exists in the mid-town area of Prosperity for a business that caters to a growing number of professional women. These executives have special needs in the purchase of their outerwear.

Our intended audience is very busy with its professional life. Yet its members still need to maintain a home environment if single, or an extended home environment if married and with children. Purchasing the kind of wardrobe their multiple lives demand requires time and patience, and usually too little of either is available after professional and domestic demands are met.

Worthmore's Fashions intends to satisfy the needs of this growing and profitable market. It is not being filled at this time in our city.

Prosperity has a growing number of business firms in the mid-town area, where many of our intended audience are working. Our planned store will attract considerable business during the middle of the day, when these women are on their lunch hours. On at least one weekday, the store will remain open until 9:00 PM to accommodate evening shoppers from the suburbs. A Sunday store-opening from 9:00 to 5:00 will also be planned, and perhaps extended, as response dictates.

Our planned store location at Main and North streets is on a convenient, well-lighted corner, accessible for day or evening traffic. Moderately-priced stores are located within a few blocks, such as *Sound Pharmacy, Kiddie Korral, Better Books, Nord Italiano Ristorante* and *Mike's Deli,* making for a good merchandise mix as well as for substantial foot traffic.

There is street parking on every adjacent street, a city parking lot one block away, and five bus routes, both local and long distance, on Main Street.

Give a quick overview of your proposal.

An estimated 37 percent return-on-investment worked out on the following financials make *Worthmore's Fashions* a sound investment and much-needed contribution to our viable community.

The experience of the proprietor-manager, combined with local opportunities, assures the long-range success of this enterprise.

Step 4 Description of Business

Product or Service

Description of Business

Worthmore's Fashions is a ladies' ready-to-wear shop that will be located at 1000 Main St. in Prosperity, Pennsylvania, a high-traffic corner that prior history has shown to enjoy optimum traffic of virtually any location in the mid-town area.

The nearest store that can be considered partially competitive is five blocks away. Ample municipal parking exists within a minute's walk. Display windows on two sides of the building offer excellent exposure of our merchandise to pedestrians. The following is a detailed description of planned merchandise:

Products

Description	Percent of Inventory
Group A—Coats	30%
Group B—Designer Coats—Off-Price	20%
Group C—Raincoats	20%
Group D—Jackets	20%
Group E—Handbags	7%
Group F—Gloves and Wallets	3%

Groups A, B and C will be 100% woolens or combinations of synthetics and will be no higher than $300 retail.

Group B (designers' coats off-price such as sample coats, discontinued styles or manufacturers' overcuts), will be purchased for cash.

Group C (raincoats) will be 100% cotton or synthetic combinations or coated nylon, an all-year-round product group.

Group D (jackets) will be 100% wool or synthetic combinations for the fall season and will be lighter material and designed for the holiday, spring or summer season.

Group E and F (handbags, gloves and wallets) will be rotated in design, materials and purpose to sell throughout the year.

Inventory and open-to-buy (the amount of funds budgeted for new purchases) will be determined by the season and the unit and dollar sales. Adequate sales with be required for good turnover of the inventory in order to have open-to-buy for new styles.

Primary Suppliers

Coats and Jackets:

Premiere Coat Manufacturer

Studio Coats, Inc.

Empire Outerwear, Inc.

Designer Coats:

St. Guerre Design, Inc.

Marie Modes, Inc.

Raincoats:

Milano London, Ltd.

Fleet Rainwear, Inc.

Customer Services

Credit Cards—VISA, MasterCard, Discover and American Express

Lay-Away—⅓ down and ⅓ each for two months

Returns—three days with sales slip

Deliveries—Free for city, normal charges elsewhere

Guarantees—30 days on manufacturers' imperfections

Complaints—24-hour recorder with return call within one
working day

Open—Weekdays from 10AM to 6PM, Friday 10AM to 9PM,
Saturday and Sunday 9AM to 5PM; appointments on call

Step 5 Market Research—
Pinpointing Customers

Prosperity's population: 150,000

Metropolitan area population: 625,000

Principal Industries: Professional and financial centers, local
government offices, a number of "clean" industries primarily in the
service, light chemical and electronic areas. All industries have proven to
be remarkably stable and recession-proof. Because of the high-percentage
of government and financial payrolls, the average income does not
fluctuate with the seasons.

Customer Base: Middle-income women, 25 to 60 years of age, earning
between $25,000 and $75,000 annually. Fifty-five percent of trading area
population is female. An equal percentage of women in the above age
range is in the local workforce.

Outside Assistance: The Chamber of Commerce and the Economic
Development Bureau and SCORE (SBA) have been immensely helpful in
providing corroborating information and research material, training and
advice, and they are available for continuing counseling. The proprietor
has attended a business startup workshop conducted by the SBDC at
Prosperity University as well as a retail management workshop offered by
SCORE. Considerable market research information was obtained from
the above organizations.

Target Market

Primary: Women between ages 25 and 60, who are employed within a 10-block radius in professional positions, are our target market. Primary customers are anticipated to be the busiest, most-highly paid, professional women who seek better clothes, more personal service and assistance, and are reliable, repeat customers.

Secondary: Women working in offices, light industries and the five commercial-industrial parks and malls within a 10-mile radius are our secondary market.

Tertiary: Visitors, tourists, and prospective customers from areas outside of the 10-mile perimeter, including men purchasing for women on special occasions.

Worthmore's Fashions will focus on professional and middle-income working women ages 25 to 60. Their estimated annual income is from $25,000 to $75,000. The majority of prospective customers work within a 10-block area of the store and are considered walk-in traffic.

Within a 10-mile radius of *Worthmore's Fashions* lie four industrial-and-office parks. Several hundred female prospects work in these facilities and efforts will be made to attract them to the store.

Considerable drive-by traffic also exists, adding to an estimated potential customer base of more than 10,000 women, of whom more than 30 percent are considered prime prospects.

Step 6 Competition

In the 10-mile radius of our location, four stores have been identified as being partially or somewhat competitive:

Smith Clothiers, well-established, 75-year-old company; large inventory of popularly-priced lines. Well-stocked on outerwear. Experienced sales help. Carries its own accounts (credit). More of a limited department store than a specialty operation.

La Femme Fantastique, in business for only two years; carries a very showy, not classic, line of styles, concentrating on dresses and sporty outfits. Limited selections, heavy turnover; youthful appeal.

Today's Woman, established three years ago as a mid-priced fashion store appealing to working and housekeeping women. Selections are not carried in depth, and inventory turnover does not appear to be fast enough to keep styles updated. Advertising reflects continuous sales. The store might present our most direct competition.

Strategy vis-a-vis Competition

Concentration on my specialty, quality outerwear for professional women; in-depth selections; middle-range pricing; exceptional personal service; unquestioned guarantees; convenient shopping hours and personal appointments are the advantages that will put *Worthmore's Fashions* into the ranks of successful local businesses. Unlike chain stores, this store will always be owner managed.

Step 7 Management

Proprietor's Experience and Goals:

I (Mary Worthmore) am a retired buyer for *Capitol Stores* in Prosperity. I have 20 years of experience, principally in the ladies' coat department. During my two decades with the above company, I have learned all facets of buying, stocking, retail store management, and floor sales. I am well-acquainted with manufacturing and purchasing, having made innumerable business trips to the major fashion centers of New York, Los Angeles, Paris, London and Tokyo. I have ongoing rapport with all major resources and received considerable encouragement to pursue this specialty business in Prosperity.

Several important vendors have agreed to set up moderate lines of credit. More details on expected credit lines and personal details are contained in the Appendix of this business plan.

Realizing the advantage of starting out with the best-available counsel to complement my pragmatic experience, I have assembled the following team to assure the success of *Worthmore's Fashions:*

Attorney .... Philip Peterson, Esq.
Prince and Associates
100 Professional Plaza, Suite 00
Prosperity, PA 15329
(814) 555-4567

Accountant .... Albert Able, CPA
Able Accounting Corp.
100 Commerce Building, Suite 00
Prosperity, PA 15329
(814) 555-8910

Banking .... George Given, VP, Branch Manager
Commerce Bank
Main and Keystone
Prosperity, PA 15329
(814) 555-1112

Insurance .... *Cover All Insurance Inc.*
Ms. P.R. Otect, Agent
100 Security Boulevard, Suite 00
Prosperity, PA 15329
(814) 555-1314

Consultants .... *Prosperity Economic Development Agency*
A.D. Vice, Director
City Hall, Room 1234
Prosperity, PA 15329
(814) 555-1516

Service Corps of Retired Executives
Mr. Paul Wiseman, Counselor
Chamber of Commerce Bldg., Suite 00
Prosperity, PA 15329
(814) 555-1718

Personnel

Personnel: During the foreseeable startup year, we plan to employ only part-time personnel, each working no more than 20 hours a week. A number of experienced saleswomen, seamstresses and interns are available to fill the needs of the store, depending on seasons and merchandising events that could require additonal help.

I do not contemplate having any partners.

Based on increase of business, my needs to make trips to the fashion markets, and availability of cash flow, permanent or full-time personnel will be considered in our second year. It is expected that our experience with numerous part-time helpers will give us a pragmatic overview of the best individuals available.

Step 8 Business Location

Location, Location, Location

The store will be located in a four-story building occupied by offices, located at the corner of Main Street and North, in the downtown office section of Prosperity. Total leasable area is 1000 sq. ft. with a large display window flanking a recessed entrance door. The entrance is a revolving door which was left in place by a previous tenant. Display windows are in acceptable condition and each equipped with dual electric floor outlets and several ceiling high-hat outlets. Additional improvements in the interior are contemplated, and the landlord, the Prosperity Improvement Corporation, has agreed to contribute $3,000 toward leasehold improvements. This amounts to approximately 50 percent of improvements I expect to make, amounting primarily to dressing rooms (2), racks, one display case (used), furnishings, desk and chairs. Additional needed electrical connections and a restroom are already in place and in acceptable condition.

Zoning permits only a frontage sign. Electric overhead connections are available on both sides of the corner store. Two elegantly-designed painted signs, illuminated by existing fixtures, will be employed.

The lease calls for 1000 sq. ft. @ $24 per sq. ft., including utilities, which has been worked out with PIC, payable at $2,000 per month for five (5) years. A renewal option for an additional five (5) years has been negotiated at no more than ten (10) percent above current rental. (Please see my copy of proposed lease in Appendix.)

Legal Structure

Mary Worthmore, doing business as *Worthmore's Fashions*, will be registered under this fictitious name and will operate as a single proprietorship. In the future, as the business grows and liability might increase, a 'Chapter S' corporation will be considered. An attorney's guidance will be sought to explore any such change in legal structure. An accountant will be consulted annually, at tax preparation time, to weigh advantages of corporate organization in relation to gross and net income.

Business Insurance

A discussion with a local insurance broker has already been held and his proposal is included in the Appendix. Insurance coverage will initially consist of three phases:

1. Fire and burglary coverage

2. Workers' Compensation

3. Customer liability coverage

Additional insurance coverage is under consideration. It will include glass breakage insurance, keyperson insurance, maintenance on electronic equipment, vehicle insurance upgrade.

Insurance is also in place for the building and external public areas, held by the PIC.

Step 9 Marketing Strategy

Based on my 20 years of experience, outside counseling and current market research, the following sales strategies will be emphasized:

• We will introduce a new concept in outerwear specialization.

• Continual contacts with the fashion markets will assure advance styling, correct colors, top quality for value, and proper coordination of accessories.

• Our publicity and promotion will emphasize our professionalism and convenient city location.

• A discounted designer line will be maintained as a magnet and promoted widely.

• A newsletter to customers will be developed to maintain regular contact, no later than the first of the following year.

Pricing requires special attention.

- The store's two corner windows will be changed weekly or more often, but decorated with only two or three selected items, dramatized with good "selling" signs and lights.

- Fashion show presentations will be explored during the six opening months, through contacts with local city and suburban women's groups, and planned for the following year.

- A system of rewards for bringing a friend or making repeat purchases will be developed later this year.

- Pre-season trunk showings will be planned for selected customers and with the cooperation of representatives of our better resources. Advance orders will be taken.

Pricing Policy

Normally, retailers in the fashion business "keystone" (*i.e.,* double the cost of an item) the first time it is offered to the public. Example: a garment costs $75 from the manufacturer, plus $2 delivery per unit. Thus the total delivered cost is $77. Thus the "keystoned" price is $154.

The retailer must take a number of expenses or "overhead" into consideration before recognizing a net profit. These expenses might include:

- Post-season markdowns

- Special sales and discounts

- Returns of merchandise

- Theft

- Commissions or incentives to salespeople

Each store will have different expenses to the above. They can amount to 10 to 30 percent. Any realistic projections must take such potential reductions in profits into consideration.

Promotion is a key element to a successful business.

In this "model store" we have set a policy of no carryover of merchandise from one season to the next. Such a policy allows the store to advertise that all fashion merchandise offered at the beginning of each season is fresh and up-to-date. The additional advantage of such a policy is that working capital will not be tied up in old inventory. It will permit the working capital to have a more favorable "open to buy" quota capital available to buy the new season's merchandise.

Most retail fashion stores must have a net profit of 30 to 40 percent in order to pay for all normal overhead or expenses. Let's translate all this into a typical retail shop example:

Cost of merchandise	$77
40% overhead expense	$31
Total cost of merchandise	$108
Full price of merchandise	$154
Total cost of goods/expense	$108
Profit at full markup	$46

If *Worthmore's Fashions* makes a profit of $46 on full sale price of $154, a profit of 30 percent is earned.

However, there are those five other expenses which cannot always be determined in advance, but which must be taken into consideration. If no markdowns are taken, no discounts given, no merchandise stolen and only normal salaries or commissions paid to salespeople, then a 30 percent profit would result. But any one of these items can substantially reduce or even wipe out the profit. You can now see that pricing is a very difficult part of the business plan creation. Knowledgeable buying of merchandise (especially seasonal merchandise), tight management, shrewd promotion and advertising, and luck will effect the ultimate profit and the Cash Flow and Profit Projections.

Promotion Plans: Opening and Continuing

Grand Opening: Saturday, 7 August, 2001 is the projected opening date. Plans for this period are detailed under *Business Goals* in the *Management Section*. Promotional and advertising efforts will consist primarily of publicity releases to all local print and electronic media. The first will go out two weeks in advance of opening; and a different one a week prior to opening. Two opening announcements will be scheduled in the society section of the major daily newspaper on the previous Sunday and following Wednesday. Both windows will have attractive Grand Opening signs, and displays will be ready 3 to 7 days ahead of opening. Invitation-style announcements will be mailed First Class to the presidents of local women's professional and social groups, at least four weeks before opening, to allow time for information to be disseminated and announced. Since this will occur in the summertime, these are not expected to have optimum effect, and will be supplemented by individual mailings to women executives and social leaders, teachers, businesses managed by women, in addition to editors, radio-TV personalities, *et al.*

Continuing Promotions: Since Grand Openings and holiday promotions usually demand a proportionately larger-than-average budget share, an investment of approximately $1000 per month in total promotional costs will be used for these two major periods. $2,000 remains to cover activities for the September–December segment.

Our counselor will be of continuing guidance during this period. With the assistance of the SBDC office at the university, two talented students have been recruited to lend assistance in creating both advertisements and direct mail pieces. A weekly advertisement of current fashion merchandise will be run in the local newspaper, each one spot-lighting a sketch, prepared by the university's art department, under the heading "What's new....at *Worthmore's Fashions.*"

Direct mail promotions will continue with the start of a monthly fashion newsletter, which we will publish. The circulation of these newsletters will increase with the growth of our mailing list. Window signs will be changed weekly with the change in fashion displays. We will handle our own decorating as long as is feasible, but will have professional help in

Study your competition.

reserve. Holiday displays will be coordinated with the Prosperity Merchants' Council, affiliated with the Chamber of Commerce. Decorations will cover the front of our store. Two small, elegantly-decorated evergreen trees will be placed in the windows, and Christmas cookies will be available within the store for five weeks prior to Christmas.

Two invitation-only "Men's Nights" will be planned for the first and second Friday evenings of December. Special holiday gift certificates will also be available at that time.

Seasonal promotions during gift-giving seasons and the promotion of executive gift certificates will also attract a select percentage of male customers.

Marketing Strategy Schedule

Time Scheduling Chart for six months Pre and Post Opening

1. Complete Installation of Fixtures

2. Take Inventory and Price-Tag Merchandise

3. Sales Training

4. Displays, Signage

5. Produce Mailers, Ads

6. Mail Promotions

7. Place Ads, Publicity

8. Pre-Opening Reception

9. Grand Opening

10. Place Thank-You Ads

11. Fill in Inventory

12. Review Sales, Selling, Personnel, Mailing List

13. Plan Holiday Ads, Promos, Decorations

14. Begin Holiday Promotion

15. Check Inventory, Plan Post-Holiday Sales

Particular emphasis will be placed on three (3) major functions:

1. Good training and observation of full and part-time sales personnel. Most employees at this time will be part-time employees.

2. Continual inventory auditing to assure full selections.

3. Diligent collection of visitors' and customers' names and addresses for promotional mailing list.

The following is an anticipated schedule for the startup of *Worthmore's Fashions.* The months between now and the opening will be devoted to buying and processing inventory; completing the installation of fixtures of the store; continuing marketing and research observation; hiring and training one or two assistants; and preparing promotional materials. Meetings with my accountant and attorney will continue as necessary.

1. Announcements to local women's organizations mailed 7 July 2001.

2. Announcements placed in local newspapers previous to and following 7 August 2001.

3. Grand Opening 7 August 2001.

4. Review of operation by 1 October 2001 and analysis of sales, data base of customers and visitors, and merchandise turnover.

5. Filling in with new merchandise, especially small-ticket holiday and gift merchandise; order holiday decor, bags, and announcements for customer prospect list, during October 2001.

6. Begin decorating and change displays for holidays; special evening

promotions starting November 15.

7. Extend evening shopping hours (depending in part on plans of merchants' association), by December 14, 2001.

8. Plan post-holiday sales event, effective December 26.

Step 10 Financial Information

The business will begin as a single proprietorship. The planned loan of $40,000 will re-invested in additional Spring lines, as our first five months of experience dictate. Collateral on my condominium, with a market value of $140,000, is expected to be $80,000 and will be used as circumstances dictate.

10.1 Capital Requirements

Proprietor's outside income from
 paid-up pension fund $10,000

Current investment
 $60,000 at 4% $2,400

Expected annual salary from store $10,000

Estimated first-year net profit before taxes,
 based upon $300,000 net sales
 and 4.0% net profit $12,000

Estimated first-year earnings from operations $22,000

Return on Investment

Total cash investment $60,000

Estimated earnings $22,000

Percentage earned (Return on Investment) .... 37 percent

Compared to current income of 4 percent on investments, the income from my planned store operation is more than nine times as high. An additional benefit is that I will have closer control over my earnings.

I am in a position to build equity in a business that might some day be worth one-times gross or some other multiple of net income.

The above figures reflect first-year projections and are expected to rise year by year, until relative market saturation is reached and expansion plans would be appropriate.

Lender Equity

I project that a line of credit of $40,000, added to personal investment capital, will provide (1) current working capital after opening expenses, paid out of personal investments; (2) provide a cushion to cover unforeseen expenses; (3) allow for addition of merchandising lines that are either in demand or that will be offered by resources, usually at favorable discounts; (4) permit marketing activities that could lead to more rapid growth.

My details of projected operating statistics are attached.

10.2 Depreciable Assets

Equipment

This section can include:

> Leasehold Improvements
> Fixturing
> Signage
> Vehicles
> Store/Office Equipment

Upon advice of counselors and in order to preserve personal equity for the purchase of current merchandise at all times, most depreciable assets will be leased rather than purchased.

Leasehold improvements to the premises of the 1000 sq. ft. store, especially window framing, entrance door, placement of electric outlets, improvements to floors and sanitary facilities, will be incorporated into the lease and amortized by the landlord over the terms of the five-year lease.

Fixtures will be purchased, but is limited to open, illuminated racks, free-standing display stands, one counter and one display case. A movable wall will separate the sales floor from the stock room where mobile racks and tables are the only fixtures needed. Some fixtures will be purchased from bankrupt stock and all will be paid from my personal funds.

Signs will consist of two overhead illuminated marquees which are being acquired on a lease-purchase-and-maintenance contract, payable in moderate monthly installments.

No vehicle will be purchased during the first month. If an additional vehicle is needed, it will be projected for the second year.

Store/Office Equipment consists of a computer which I presently own and which will be installed in the store for purposes of maintaining inventory and customer records. An electronic cash register that also processes credit cards, maintains inventory control and calculates cash flow will be leased. No other equipment is contemplated to be acquired or leased at this time.

10.3 Starting Balance Sheet

Assets and Liabilities of Mary Worthmore
as of 31 January 2001

Assets

Current Assets

Investment no. 1	$1,625
Investment no. 2	$6,275
Investment no. 3	$60,000
Investment no. 4	$40,000
Investment no. 5	$21,500
Total Current Assets	$129,400

Fixed Assets

Condominium	$150,000
Furniture and Decorations	$16,000
Automobile	$10,000
Total Fixed Assets	$176,000

Total Assets $305,400

Liabilities

Current Liabilities

Condominium Mortgage	$440
Condominium Tax Payment	$120
Condominium Maintenance Fee	$85
Credit Cards	$60
Total Current Liabilities	$705

Fixed Liabilities

Mortgage Balance	$65,000
Total Fixed Liabilities	$65,000

Total Liabilities $65,705

Total Net Worth $239,695
(i.e., Total Assets less Total Liabilities)

Total Net Worth + Liabilities $305,400

Monthly Budget

of Mary Worthmore
31 January 2001

Fixed Monthly Expenses...

Mortgage Condominium	$440
Condominium Fee	$85
Condominium Taxes	$120
Health Plan	$120
Life Insurance	$30
Condominium Insurance	$20
Auto Insurance	$50
Auto Registration	$6
Estimated Taxes	$200
Total Fixed Monthly Expenses	**$1,071**

Controllable (*i.e.*, variable) Expenses

Telephone	$30
Gas & Electricity	$45
Food	$120
Credit Card Payments	$80
Restaurant & Outside Eating	$50
Auto Gas & Maintenance	$42
Laundry & Cleaning	$20

Dentists	$25
Newspapers & Publications	$15
Miscellaneous	$50
Gifts & Contributions	$20
Total Controllable Expenses	**$497**
Grand Total Expenses	**$1,568**

Monthly Income...

Pension	$1,000
Bank Account Interest ($1600 @ 3%)	$4
Investment #1 ($6277 @ 3.25%)	$17
Investment #2 ($60,000 @ 6%)	$300
Investment #3 ($40,000 @ 6.5%)	$217
Investment #4 ($31,360 @ 7.5%)	$196
Investment #5 ($21,460 @ 8.5%)	$152
Total Personal Income	**$1,886**
(less) Expenses	**-$1,568**
Net Personal Income	**$318**

10.4 Break-Even Analysis

Financial Management

Attached hereto are financials based on our projections for the fiscal year 2002. Figures are based on our educated estimates, national averages typical for our business, and consultations with both paid and volunteer professionals.

The figures are conservative.

I would like to point out that the Cash Flow Projected Statement shows a positive cash flow. These figures can be accomplished with existing financial resources and agreements with major resources to postpone billing (60-to-90-day dating).

However, the requested loan of $40,000 is necessary as a safeguard to cover unexpected and unforeseen operating expenses, to assure payment of fall and winter merchandise, to facilitate the cash purchase of designer fashion merchandise at advantageous prices, and to weather any possible volume decline after the holidays. An upswing in sales is expected traditionally during the spring and Easter period to compensate for winter lulls and post-season markdowns.

The cost of carrying the loan, repayments and interest, will be assured by the traditional spring-Easter sales increases. Also, it is expected that favorable holiday business will allow a healthy residue of assets to be present. The loan, however, is insurance for a progressive and profitable operation.

Company Name:

Worthmore's Fashions

Break-Even-Point Worksheet
Period From 1 August 2001 to 31 July 2002

Fixed Expenses

1. Rent (15)*		$24,000
2. Insurance (16)*		$5,100
3. License/Tax		$1,800
4. Loan Payments		$7,488
5. Depreciation (23)*		$1,404
6. Interest Expense		
7. Professional Fees (Acctg/Legal, *et al.*)		$2,700
8. Owner's Salary (4)*		$10,000
9. Other		
10. <u>Total Fixed Expenses</u>		<u>$52,492</u>

Variable Expenses

11. Direct Material

12. Direct Labor

13. Overhead or Other Costs

14. Variable Expenses (2)* $180,000
(cost of sales)

Semi-Variable or Semi-Fixed

15. Sales Salaries (5)* $17,100

16. Payroll Taxes (6)* $3,420

17. Advertising (7)* $15,000

18. Store Supplies (8)* $3,250

19. Auto Expense (9)* $2,300

20. Traveling (10)* $6,000

21. Telephone (11)* $1,550

22. Utilities (12)* $2,430

23. Miscellaneous (14)*-line 7 $3,980
    line 13 on income projection statement
    minus line 7 from page 101)

24. Other

25. **Total Semi-Variable and Semi-Fixed** $55,030

Recapitulation of break-even point worksheet line numbers

26. Fixed Expenses—line 10 $52,492

27. 50% of Semi-Var—line 25 $27,515

28. **Total Fixed Expenses** $80,007

29. Variable Expense—line 14 $180,000

30. 50% of Semi-Var—line 25 $27,515

31. **Total Variable Expenses** $207,515
    (*i.e.*, line 29 + line 30)

32. Grand Total Expenses $287,522
(i.e., line 28 + line 31)

33. Total profit before taxes (26)* $12,478

34. <u>Net Sales</u> (1)*   <u>$300,000</u>

35. Percent of total sales revenue required to break even = 86.5%
(i.e., line 28 ÷ (line 28 + line 33), specifically:

$80,007 ÷ ($80,007 + $12,478) = $80,007 ÷ $92,478 = 86.5%

36. Sales volume required to break even = $259,500
(i.e., line 34 x line 35)

37. Average *monthly* sales required to break even = $21,625
(i.e., line 36 ÷ 12 months)

*Note: Above numbers in parentheses (in left column) correspond to line numbers on the Income Statement on the following page.

WORTHMORE'S FASHIONS
INCOME PROJECTION STATEMENT

PERIOD: FISCAL YEAR August 1, 2001 to July 31, 2002

	Industry Average	WORTHMORE'S FASHIONS	1 Aug	2 Sep	3 Oct	4 Nov	5 Dec	6 Jan	7 Feb	8 Mar	9 Apr	10 May	11 Jun	12 Jul	TOTAL YEAR
1. Net Sales	100.0%	100.0%	$30,000	$32,000	$38,000	$40,000	$30,000	$15,000	$15,000	$16,000	$18,000	$19,000	$22,000	$25,000	$300,000
2. Cost of Sales	59.1%	60.0%	18,000	19,200	22,800	24,000	18,000	9,000	9,000	9,600	10,800	11,400	13,200	15,000	180,000
3. GROSS PROFIT (1-2)	40.9%	40.0%	$12,000	$12,800	$15,200	$16,000	$12,000	$6,000	$6,000	$6,400	$7,200	$7,600	$8,800	$10,000	$120,000
OPERATING EXPENSES Controllable Variable Expense															
4. Owner's Withdrawal	5.0%	3.3%	$0	$0	$0	$1,111	$1,112	$1,111	$1,111	$1,111	$1,111	$1,111	$1,111	$1,111	$10,000
5. Salaries	8.9%	5.7%	1,800	1,800	1,800	1,800	1,500	1,200	1,200	1,200	1,200	1,200	1,200	1,200	17,100
6. Payroll Taxes	1.9%	1.1%	360	360	360	360	300	240	240	240	240	240	240	240	3,420
7. Advertising	2.2%	5.0%	2,000	1,200	1,200	1,200	1,000	1,200	1,200	1,200	1,200	1,200	1,200	1,200	15,000
8. Store Supplies	2.1%	1.1%	500	250	250	250	250	250	250	250	250	250	250	250	3,250
9. Auto Expense	0.8%	0.8%	300	200	200	200	150	150	150	150	200	200	200	200	2,300
10. Travel	0.7%	2.0%	1,200	600	600	600	0	600	0	600	0	600	600	600	6,000
11. Telephone	0.5%	0.5%	200	150	150	150	150	150	100	100	100	100	100	100	1,550
12. Utilities	1.3%	0.8%	190	200	200	225	225	225	225	200	180	180	180	200	2,430
13. Miscellaneous	2.0%	2.2%	1,200	640	760	880	600	300	300	320	360	380	440	500	6,680
14. TOTAL VARIABLE EXPENSES (Sum of 4 to 13)	25.4%	22.6%	$7,750	$5,400	$5,520	$6,776	$5,287	$5,426	$4,776	$5,371	$4,841	$5,461	$5,521	$5,601	$67,730
FIXED EXPENSES (OVERHEAD)															
15. Rent	8.9%	8.0%	$2,000	$2,000	$2,000	$2,000	$2,000	$2,000	$2,000	$2,000	$2,000	$2,000	$2,000	$2,000	$24,000
16. Insurance	1.4%	1.7%	425	425	425	425	425	425	425	425	425	425	425	425	5,100
17. Taxes	0.6%	0.6%	180	192	228	240	180	90	90	96	108	114	132	150	1,800
18. TOTAL FIXED EXPENSES (Sum of 15 to 17)	10.9%	10.3%	$2,605	$2,617	$2,653	$2,665	$2,605	$2,515	$2,515	$2,521	$2,533	$2,539	$2,557	$2,575	$30,900
19. TOTAL EXPENSES (14 + 18)	36.3%	32.9%	$10,355	$8,017	$8,173	$9,441	$7,892	$7,941	$7,291	$7,892	$7,374	$8,000	$8,078	$8,176	$98,630
20. NET OPERATING PROFIT (3 - 19)	4.6%	7.1%	$1,645	$4,783	$7,027	$6,559	$4,108	($1,941)	($1,291)	($1,492)	($174)	($400)	$722	$1,824	$21,370
Other Income															
21. INTEREST INCOME	1.1%	0.0%													
Other Expenses															
22. Loan Payment	-2.5%		$624	$624	$624	$624	$624	$624	$624	$624	$624	$624	$624	$624	$7,488
23. Depreciation	0.5%	0.5%	$117	$117	$117	$117	$117	$117	$117	$117	$117	$117	$117	$117	$1,404
24. Interest Expense	0.5%														
25. TOTAL OTHER (21 - 22 to 24)	0.4%	-3.0%	$741	$741	$741	$741	$741	$741	$741	$741	$741	$741	$741	$741	$8,892
26. TOTAL PROFIT BEFORE TAXES (20- or +25)	4.2%	4.2%	$904	$4,042	$6,286	$5,818	$3,367	($2,682)	($2,032)	($2,233)	($915)	($1,141)	($19)	$1,083	$12,478
27. INCOME TAXES															
28. NET PROFIT OR (LOSS) AFTER INCOME TAXES (26-27)															

WORTHMORE'S FASHIONS
MONTHLY CASH FLOW PROJECTION

	Start-up Position	2001 1 Aug	2 Sep	3 Oct	4 Nov	5 Dec	2002 6 Jan	7 Feb	8 Mar	9 Apr	10 May	11 Jun	12 Jul	TOTAL
1. CASH ON HAND	$60,000	$63,150	$53,171	$60,766	$69,808	$76,083	$72,627	$60,602	$57,977	$55,889	$55,695	$54,438	$55,692	$58,026
2. CASH RECEIPTS														
a. Cash Sales		12,000	12,800	15,200	16,000	12,000	6,000	6,000	6,400	7,200	7,600	8,800	10,000	120,000
b. Credit Card Collections		18,000	19,200	22,800	24,000	18,000	9,000	9,000	9,600	10,800	11,400	13,200	15,000	180,000
c. Loan or Other Cash In	40,000		3,000											3,000
3. TOTAL CASH RECEIPTS (2a+2b+2c=3)	$40,000	$30,000	$35,000	$38,000	$40,000	$30,000	$15,000	$15,000	$16,000	$18,000	$19,000	$22,000	$25,000	$303,000
4. TOTAL CASH AVAILABLE (1+3=4)	$100,000	$93,150	$88,171	$98,766	$109,808	$106,083	$87,627	$75,602	$73,977	$73,889	$74,695	$76,438	$80,692	$361,026
5. CASH PAID OUT														
a. Purchases (Merchandise)	$11,000	$29,000	$18,000	$19,200	$22,800	$24,000	$18,000	$9,000	$9,000	$9,600	$10,800	$11,400	$13,200	$194,000
b. Salaries (Excludes withdrawals)	250	1,800	1,800	1,800	1,800	1,500	1,200	1,200	1,200	1,200	1,200	1,200	1,200	17,100
c. Payroll Taxes	50	360	360	360	360	300	240	240	240	240	240	240	240	3,420
d. Advertising	1,500	2,000	1,200	1,200	1,200	1,100	1,100	1,200	1,200	1,200	1,200	1,200	1,200	15,000
e. Supplies (Office & Store)	500	500	250	250	250	250	250	250	250	250	250	250	250	3,250
f. Auto Expense	300	300	200	200	200	150	150	150	150	200	200	200	200	2,300
g. Travel	2,000	1,200	600	600	600	0	600	0	600	0	600	600	600	6,000
h. Telephone	200	200	150	150	150	150	150	100	100	100	100	100	100	1,550
i. Utilities	190	190	200	200	225	225	225	225	200	180	180	180	200	2,430
j. Miscellaneous – Opening	2,775	1,200	640	760	880	600	300	300	320	360	380	440	500	6,680
k. Rent	2,000	2,000	2,000	2,000	2,000	2,000	2,000	2,000	2,000	2,000	2,000	2,000	2,000	24,000
l. Insurance	425	425	425	425	425	425	425	425	425	425	425	425	425	5,100
m. Repairs & Maintenance				125		100		150			225			600
n. Accounting & Legal	350		200	200	200	200	200	200	200	200	200	200	200	2,200
o. Credit Card Fees			576	684	720	540	270	270	288	324	342	396	436	4,846
p. Real Estate, etc.	180	180	180	180	180	180	180	180	180	180	180	180	180	2,160
q. Interest														
r. Subtotal (5a thru 5q)	$20,650	39,355	26,781	28,334	31,990	31,720	25,290	15,890	16,353	16,459	18,522	19,011	20,931	290,636
s. Loan Payments		$624	$624	$624	$624	$624	$624	$624	$624	$624	$624	$624	$624	$7,488
t. Capital Purchases (Name)	8,000													
u. Other Start-Up Costs	6,000													
v. Reserve or Escrow (Name)	2,200													
w. Owner's Withdrawal					1,111	1,112	1,111	1,111	1,111	1,111	1,111	1,111	1,111	10,000
6. TOTAL CASH PAID OUT (5a thru 5w)	$36,850	39,979	27,405	28,958	33,725	33,456	27,025	17,625	18,088	18,194	20,257	20,746	22,666	308,124
7. CASH POSITION (End of Month) (4 minus 6)	$63,150	53,171	60,766	69,808	76,083	72,627	60,602	55,889	55,695	54,438	55,692	58,026		

105

WORTHMORE'S FASHIONS
ANNUAL CASH FLOW PROJECTION
Period: FISCAL YEARS 2001 thru 2003

	Year 1 FY 2001	Year 2 FY 2002	Year 3 FY 2003
1. CASH ON HAND	$58,026	$52,902	$64,114
2. CASH RECEIPTS			
a. Cash Sales	120,000	140,000	160,000
b. Credit Card Collections	180,000	210,000	240,000
c. Loan or Other Cash In	3,000	0	0
3. TOTAL CASH RECEIPTS (2a+2b+2c=3)	303,000	350,000	400,000
4. TOTAL CASH AVAILABLE (1+3=4)	361,026	402,902	464,114
5. CASH PAID OUT			
a. Purchases (Merchandise)	194,000	210,000	240,000
b. Salaries (Excludes Withdrawals)	17,100	19,000	22,000
c. Payroll Taxes	3,420	3,800	4,400
d. Advertising	15,000	16,000	18,000
e. Store Supplies	3,250	3,350	3,500
f. Auto Expense	2,300	2,500	2,700
g. Travel	6,000	7,500	8,000
h. Telephone	1,550	1,650	1,700
i. Utilities	2,430	2,600	2,700
j. Miscellaneous—Opening	6,680	4,400	4,000
k. Rent	24,000	24,000	24,000
l. Insurance	5,100	5,100	5,300
m. Repairs & Maintenance	600	800	1,000
n. Accounting & Legal	2,200	2,500	3,000
o. Credit Card Fees	4,846	6,300	7,200
p. Real Estate, etc.	2,160	1,800	2,000
q. Interest	0	0	0
r. Subtotal (5a thru 5q)	290,636	311,300	349,500
s. Loan Payments	7,480	7,488	7,488
t. Capital Purchases (Name)	0	0	1,000
u. Other Start-Up Costs	0	0	0
v. Reserve or Escrow (Name)	0	0	0
w. Owner's Withdrawal	10,000	20,000	30,000
6. TOTAL CASH PAID OUT (5a thru 5w)	308,124	338,788	387,988
7. CASH POSITION (End of year) (4 minus 6)	$52,902	$64,114	$76,126

106

WORTHMORE'S FASHIONS
INCOME PROJECTION STATEMENT

PERIOD: FISCAL YEARS 2001 thru 2003

	Industry Average	Fiscal Year 2001		Fiscal Year 2002		Fiscal Year 2003	
1. Net Sales	100.0%	$300,000	100.0%	$350,000	100%	$400,000	100.0%
2. Cost of Sales	59.1%	180,000	60%	210,000	60%	240,000	60%
3. GROSS PROFIT (1-2)	40.9%	120,000	40%	140,000	40%	160,000	40%
OPERATING EXPENSES Controllable Variable Expense							
4. Owner's Withdrawal	5.0%	10,000	3.3%	20,000	5.7%	30,000	7.5%
5. Salaries	8.9%	17,100	5.7%	19,000	5.4%	22,000	5.5%
6. Payroll Taxes	1.9%	3,420	1.1%	3,800	1.1%	4,400	1.1%
7. Advertising	2.2%	15,000	5.0%	16,000	4.6%	18,000	4.5%
8. Store Supplies	2.1%	3,250	1.1%	3,350	1.0%	3,500	0.9%
9. Auto Expense	0.8%	2,300	0.8%	2,500	0.7%	2,700	0.7%
10. Travel	0.7%	6,000	2.0%	7,500	2.1%	8,000	2.0%
11. Telephone	0.5%	1,550	0.5%	1,650	0.5%	1,700	0.4%
12. Utilities	1.3%	2,430	0.8%	2,600	0.7%	2,700	0.7%
13. Miscellaneous	2.0%	6,680	2.2%	7,700	2.2%	8,000	2.0%
14. TOTAL VARIABLE EXPENSES (Sum of 4 to 13)	25.4%	67,730	22.6%	84,100	24.0%	101,000	25.3%
FIXED EXPENSES (OVERHEAD)							
15. Rent	8.9%	24,000	8.0%	24,000	6.9%	24,000	6.0%
16. Insurance	1.4%	5,100	1.7%	5,100	1.5%	5,300	1.3%
17. Taxes	0.6%	1,800	0.6%	1,800	0.5%	2,000	0.5%
18. TOTAL FIXED EXPENSES (Sum of 15 to 17)	10.9%	30,900	10.3%	30,900	8.8%	31,300	7.8%
19. TOTAL EXPENSES (14 + 18)	36.3%	98,630	32.9%	115,000	32.9%	132,300	33.1%
20. NET OPERATING PROFIT (3 - 19)	4.6%	21,370	7.1%	25,000	7.1%	27,700	6.9%
Other Income							
21. INTEREST INCOME	1.1%		0.0%		0.0%		0.0%
Other Expenses							
22. Loan Payment	1.0%	7,488	-2.5%	7,488	-2.1%	7,488	-1.9%
23. Depreciation	0.5%	1,404	-0.5%	1,404	-0.4%	1,604	-0.4%
24. Interest Income	-0.4%						
25. TOTAL OTHER [21 - (22 to 24)]		8,892	-3.0%	8,892	-2.5%	9,092	-2.3%
26. TOTAL PROFIT BEFORE TAXES (20- or +25)	4.2%	$12,478	4.2%	$16,108	4.6%	$18,608	4.7%
27. INCOME TAXES							
28. NET PROFIT OR (LOSS) AFTER INCOME TAXES (26-27)							

Step 11: Record Keeping

My existing personal computer will be used to utilize an accrual book-keeping system. My experience in computer operation will enable me to perform all day-by-day bookkeeping tasks on a weekly basis. An accountant will prepare quarterly and annual taxes. An electronic terminal will maintain perpetual inventory, allow at least eight (8) group entries, separate sales tax, cash sales, and credit card sales. I expect that a large percentage of sales will be made by debit or credit cards. While this method adds a few percentage points to the cost of doing business, it will enable me to recoup cash more quickly, eliminate the need for credit sales (except layaways), and avoid collection costs and potential losses.

Credit card sales: Prior to opening I will set up a Credit Card Merchant Account arrangement with the bank.

I will keep a database of all sales, noting customers' names, addresses, phone numbers, and other vital particulars. Such records will enable us to make follow-up contacts and develop a valuable mailing list, as well as personalize our relations with each customer.

Chapter IV

Secrets of Financing

How to Get a Loan and What to Do if You Are Turned Down

Using Your Business Plan to Get a Loan

The most brilliant and professional business plan remains a bunch of printed papers unless you understand the nature of the person who is going to look it over and make a judgment, and decide or recommend that a loan is extended to you. The psychology of getting a loan, if this is the principal purpose of your business plan, is virtually as important as its physical proposal.

Let us take a look at that loan officer and examine what he or she will be looking for.

Bear in mind that *The Lender* is a fellow businessperson whose business it is to lend money at a specific interest rate, and to take measures to ensure that his (or her!) company is repaid with interest. His livelihood depends on the successful conclusion of your loan application. The overriding constraint he has on approving your loan is his concern that you might be unable to repay his institution's loan. With thousands of bank and savings & loan bankruptcies occurring annually, loan officers are understandably cautious. Given those legitimate concerns of your lender, you should devote an appropriate measure of thoroughness and thoughtfulness to your business plan to address and allay those concerns.

> *The loan officer's livelihood depends upon the successful conclusion of your loan application.*

Once you have completed your business plan and checked it for accuracy in spelling and figures, you need to sit back and think of yourself once more. Let's critique your request.

Question number one: Is the amount of your loan request (or credit line) sufficient to accommodate all possible reverses, unexpected slowdowns or expansions? Or is it too much? Perhaps you do not need as much as you are asking. Remember that you must earn the money you will need to pay back the loan—plus interest.

Question number two: While you are thoroughly steeped in your business, does your business plan reflect this conviction and enthusiasm? The lender on the other side of the desk does not share your knowledge about your enterprise, nor your conviction that it will succeed, nor your belief that your business is unique and everyone will beat a path to your door. The lender (1) wants to know every minute detail about your business until he knows almost as much about it as you do, (2) needs to catch your excitement until he, too, believes in its unequivocal success, and (3) has seen all kinds of other business plans and might not share your viewpoint of its exclusivity.

Consider all of these probabilities and then proceed to the "psychology" of making your business plan presentation.

The management of your new business or expanding business is of primary importance to the success of the enterprise as well as your loan application. We have offered pointers on this topic elsewhere in this book, but we cannot reiterate this importance too often. you are the creator; you are the reason for the business's being and continuance; you are the bearer of the business plan and loan application; and you are the one who is charged with the payback of the loan. So here is a quick 10-point check list again to use as a last-minute review before you enter the bank or financial institution with your business plan in hand:

1. **Your Appearance:** The way you look during your interview is the way you are likely to be judged. The lending officer is very likely to be conservatively dressed. He will feel more comfortable with someone who is similarly dressed. Remember that first appearances are important.

You must earn enough to pay back your loan— plus interest.

2. **Documents:** Check and double-check to make sure all needed documents are available quickly and easily. It will show your thoroughness, your organizing ability, and eliminate any nervousness on your part.

3. **The Interview:** For most of us, being interviewed by a bank or financial officer is not an everyday experience. It can be a strain. Be confident, and you will be if you have prepared yourself thoroughly. Remember that you are the customer. The banker needs you, too.

4. **Questions and Answers:** Hopefully all of the bank officer's questions will be answered by your business plan. If verbal answers are necessary, give the answers with confidence and candidness. If you do not have a rational answer or are unsure, it will be better to say that you can have the answer shortly.

5. **Leading the Interview:** Do not be afraid to ask questions of your own, or to fill in any gaps in the presentation. Let your own comments reflect your enthusiasm and knowledge, without being overbearing or pompous. After all, the banker should know that you are an entrepreneur and not a messenger boy.

6. **Ask for the Loan:** Just like a sales situation should always end in a request for the order or signature, the purpose of making the presentation is to get a loan or line of credit. End your presentation with *"Do you feel that your bank can make the $xxxxx loan to my business?"*

7. **The Negative:** Bankers, particularly during these times, are just as likely to say 'no' as 'yes.' The banker might not be comfortable or able to tell you the reason for a refusal. But if you ask a direct question in a friendly way, ask him if there was a specific section in your business plan that led to the refusal. If you cannot correct the problem with this lender, then at least you can make a correction when seeing another financial institution.

8. **The Positive:** Should you be lucky the first time around and get a 'yes' from the banker, it will be your turn to assure that this loan is indeed in your best interest. Consider the amount of the loan, the interest rate, the payback period, any restrictions, the requested collateral or

> *Reflect your own enthusiasm and knowledge without being overbearing or pompous.*

any other detail in the small print. Request that you take the loan agreement with you for 24 hours in order to study it or go over it with your accountant or attorney. Then if it meets with your needs sign it and return it.

9. **Friends and Family:** Many loans are made with people close to you. This does not eliminate or reduce the responsibility that you are assuming, nor the payback. Make sure everything is in writing and is understood by both parties. It is not just the businesslike and legal way to do it, but the ethical way. Losing a friend or the support of family could be worse than not getting the money.

10. **Persistency:** In the final analysis, persistence must be part of the loan process. Like a salesman, you need to be tenacious in your efforts. The better your business plan, the more likely your success. But in case a lender, friend or family member turns you down, don't be downcast. Know and understand why you are turned down by putting yourself in the other person's shoes and try another one.

Getting a loan is a form of combat. In combat you must 1) have the proper ammunition; 2) aim at the correct target, and 3) have a cause you have a passion for.

In this analogy, 1) your ammunition is the data you gather for your business plan; 2) the correct target is your own objectives you condense into your business plan, which should simultaneously take into account the objectives and psychology of your lender, and 3) you must believe in your cause just as passionately.

Everything You've Always Wanted to Know about Your Bank But Were Afraid to Ask

Getting a loan or a line of credit is fully 50 percent of the reason for the business plan. The financial section of the business plan is, of course, for your own guidance, but it is absolutely mandatory if your own cash reserves are inadequate to launch, operate and expand your business.

Elsewhere we have offered various hints on how to produce the "financials" necessary for the Plan, and pointed to numerous pitfalls that can crop up and how to avoid them. In this chapter we take a look inside the banking business, listen in on what bankers say, and what their customers have done to cope with the banks' traditional intransigence.

The banking crises of the past decade must be borne in mind, as a partial explanation, in order to understand the traditional reluctance of banks to lend money carelessly, or on terms that we feel are acceptable and digestible. Still, as the saying goes, there is always more than one way to skin a cat.

From these examples we can learn that techniques exist (call them "psychological warfare") which can either overcome traditional banking objections or get around them with more innovative methods. As one banker said: *"We're not like venture capitalists. We're like a car rental company. When they rent you a car, they charge you for usage, and they expect to get the car back. When we give you a loan, we charge interest, and we expect to get our money back."*

When communicating with your bank before, during and after a financial transaction, remember you need to communicate on all levels. Financial transactions are not always cut-and-dried. From the bank president to the assistant loan officers, these men and women are human. Plan periodic get-togethers with them, either at your business or the bank. Candidly advise them on what you are doing, and especially on how you are using the money you have borrowed. Find out, too, how the bank's portfolio is changing from period to period. It might affect your next transaction to know fiscal or physical changes that are about to take place.

Banking Hints

The New Failure Syndrome. The profusion of bank failures around the world has indubitably spooked the banking industry. But the same goes for the customer. If your business is blessed with a sound cash position, never put all your eggs into one basket. If you have more liquid assets than that at any one time, be sure to spread it around into different banking institutions. Before depositing large amounts, either you or your accountant should check the bank's past four statements. Check to see whether the bank was profitable during the past year, carries a three percent or better ratio of net worth to assets, and a satisfactory report about who the bank is loaning major money to.

A Worst-Case Scenario. It shouldn't happen, but occasionally it does: your bank goes bankrupt. You've got money holed up in the institution. What about the loan you have with this bank? Can you walk away from your debt? No way. The government probably takes over and you still must pay back everything, just as before, to the new management. In fact, the situation could get worse. The government agency does not know you as well as your former banker does. A review by some bureaucrat might lead him (or her) to conclude that your collateral is inadequate and you will be asked for additional collateral, a co-signer, or to accelerate your payments. Dealing with the government agency is no picnic. As Gertrude Stein said, *"A debt is a debt is a debt…"*

Expanding Your Credit. We hope this will happen to you: your business expands; your present banking resource is limited, especially the credit your current bank has allocated to you. What to do? Expand by exploring an additional banking relationship. As your business expands and your credit needs increase, this should be part of your planning. Remember that the more you need to borrow to accommodate your expanding business, the greater the possibility of a turn-down from your present resource and the longer the review process. Send your financials to the loan officers of other banks, as your needs expand. Get acquainted with them before your need becomes acute.

Personal Asset Protection. Unless it is absolutely necessary to obtain needed opening or expansion capital, never pledge your personal assets, such as your residence. There is an alternative, however: get a separate loan on your private assets. Let's say you own a home with substantial equity in it. You have business property or equipment that can back a business loan. However, you need another long-term loan for additional money. Using your home equity, you could make a personal or equity loan for up to 30 years. Whereas a business loan would be written for one, two or three years, with a correspondingly high monthly payback, a personal or home equity loan, payable over a long period of time, is a much more comfortable transaction. First, second or equity home loans to support a business venture make your personal residence at risk, of course, but you are the best judge as to your chances for success. Because it is unlikely that your commercial loan officer will suggest such a split arrangement, you need to be apprised of this possibility. At this specific point in time, the reduction of monthly payments by stretching out the loan might be just what you need, at least until the business develops and generates the needed profits.

Key Executives to the Front. If yours is the kind of business that has several key executives or partners, you might consider taking turns talking to, and negotiating with, the bank's loan officers. Perhaps this will reduce your ego a bit, make you less important with the banker, but the psychology is useful. By alternating discussions and contacts, you show the bank that you have a team, and that the business is not in jeopardy if something should happen to you. Show that your business has several key players, all singing the same tune.

Other Banking Services. When dealing with a bank, you need to consider that this institution has many other services on which they make money. One of the questions your loan officer will no doubt ask you, *"Do you have any other accounts in this bank?"* He will be looking at other income opportunities from you. Do you have a safety deposit box? Do you use any of the bank's personal services? Do you have a mortgage or auto loan with the bank, any deposits or a trust arrangement? Consider what other services the bank offers you and act upon them before you consider asking for a business loan.

Play the Field. Dealing exclusively with one bank officer is not advisable. Bank officers, like so many other executives, tend to play musical chairs with their jobs. The man with whom you have established a great relationship, after many months of cultivating him, has suddenly been shifted to another office out-of-town, or joined another bank. However, his former assistant is still there and has, perhaps, been moved up into the number one slot. But the assistant knows you only as a name, and perhaps as a face. You have to become acquainted with him or her all over again unless, of course, you have taken the time and trouble to become friendly with the number two person ahead of time. Like making a political contribution, spread your attention around. You never can tell...

Educating the Loan Officer. It would be impossible to assume that the banker who is considering your loan application will be intimately familiar with your specific business or profession. Perhaps a little personal education is appropriate. Bring him a pamphlet about your company, a publicity clipping about you or your product, a sample of whatever you produce. If something is printed about your business in the local news-paper or a recognizable trade journal, it immediately assumes the nature of gospel truth. Why not take advantage of this, especially if the publicity might cost only one postage stamp? If you have something to blow your horn about, make sure the banker hears it too.

Hedging Your Bet. One executive proposes that if your collateral and reputation allow a loan or credit line of, let's say, $100,000, take this credit but never use more than half or three-quarters of it (unless, of course, you need it all). The psychology is that the banker, looking at your record, will see that you have not taken all you could take and he'll be asking you why you don't want more. Or he'll offer you a larger credit line or loan. That's the way it is in banking. Similarly, if you have adequate cash flow and can reduce the loan balance ahead of time, the banker will wonder if you don't need more money. Business people who are in such an enviable position admit that they will occasionally play this game deliberately. Psychology plays as important a part in the loan process as accounting.

Get acquainted with your banker before your need becomes acute.

Banking Is a Business. A moderate-size contractor had expanded after a number of years and was ready to make a major move, requiring a temporary infusion of cash. Because the business had a sound operating and credit history, the owner was able to come up with an impressive business plan. He submitted it to four local banks with a specific loan request. A cover letter was attached to each business plan that contained a brief postscript: *"The best bid wins."* The owner had the confidence of his convictions and told the prospective lenders up front that his business was worthwhile getting. When all "bids" were in, he selected the lowest bidder and saved thousands of dollars.

Belt-and-Suspenders. Sometimes it will appear to you that loan officers want too much security especially when they ask for personal assets to secure the business loan. It's the same mentality that wears a belt, then secures his pants further with suspenders. You must realize that it is the bank officer's job to secure as much collateral as possible. This is especially true during the past few years. However, it is your job to try and negotiate a loan most favorable to your business—particularly a loan that you can live with, pay for, and that does the job your business plan says it should. Alternatives to such bank demands could be (1) come up with more collateral; (2) reduce the amount of money you actually need or switch it to a staged line of credit; (3) offer key-man insurance that will assure the lender that, should anything happen to you, your policy will pay off the balance immediately; and (4) document your own investment in the business and your willingness to increase your equity.

Just as your business plan will tell everything about you, your business and your plans for the future, so will certain information that you can gather about the bank. Don't be afraid to ask for it. Much of it is open to the interested public. And the more you know about the bank, the better your chance for swinging a loan that you can live with.

If Your Loan Application Is Rejected

Large banks have a bad habit of turning down many loans they deem too small, too risky, inadequately collateralized or because they don't know you well enough.

Smaller banks are often more eager to do business with you, especially if they know you better, and are satisfied with smaller loans because of their lower overhead.

There is still another option: one of the hundreds of foreign-owned banks. These foreign banks some times have not been as hard hit as your local banks on bad loans, low returns on loans from big borrowers, and stringent new regulatory constraints. This situation may create opportunities for many banks that are seeking to expand their commercial banking operations.

You might want to consider taking your business plan to the officer of such a foreign bank. It is unlikely that you will need an interpreter, just the kind of credible, complete business plan you should be able to compile with the help of this guidebook.

Recent Developments on Dealing with Banks

One of the primary purposes of the business plan is to use it as leverage for a business loan or line of credit.

Dealing with banks today is a whole different ballgame than it was during previous years. You need to know the ins and outs of the banking business before you even go through the door of the first lending institution. Here are some hints from inside the banking profession:

1. Not all banks are born alike. To find the right one that will work with you and most likely authorize a loan, ask around. Question other business people in town, at the chamber of commerce, in your civic club, especially friends in the same business or profession.

2. The people who will look over your business plan and talk to you are individuals, not institutions. They represent institutions, but they still have their own personalities, idiosyncrasies, and standards. If you cannot get anywhere with one, for whatever reason, try another one, preferably at another bank. Besides, bankers are on "career tracks" and move around to different jobs. The one you talk to today might not be one who is there tomorrow.

3. Large banks are conservative. Consider applications with small to medium-size banks.

4. Banks render services beyond money lending. If you find a bank or lender who will suggest other services, or respond constructively to your inquiry, grab him as a golden resource. Some of the collateral service might include alternative methods of financing, lending and factoring advice.

5. If you get a turndown, find out why. Chances are that your accounting data is inadequate, or your collateral appears insufficient, or a nearby competitive or other challenging situation exists, known to the banker but perhaps unknown to you, that could affect the health of your loan. The closer your relationship with the bank and the banker, the better

The more you know about your bank, the better your chances for a loan.

119

your chances. Although your business plan evidences your Know-How, you still need Know-Who to complete the deal.

6. Be visible to your banker. Not all banking and lending relations can be reduced to dollars and cents. If you have dealt with the bank for some time, have other accounts there, and get to know some other employees of the institution, you'll smooth the way to the loan application and approval.

7. Present lending standards are much tougher than they were in the past. However, the two basic questions that bank officers ask remain the same: Can the business generate the cash to pay back the loan? Does the loan need collateral, and if so, is it available? Your business plan can go a long way in answering these two concerns.

Underscoring all advice from the banking industry is the need for persistency, supported by a realistic, updated business plan.

Commenting on personal guarantees expected of small businesses, both proprietorships and closely-held corporations, a senior VP stated:

> *"If a principal isn't willing to give his personal guarantee as an act of faith in the company, we certainly are not going to do business with him."*

A loan applicant's record of accomplishments, reputation and managerial skills are paramount criteria in evaluating the loan request, regardless how brilliant the business plan. One chief financial officer expressed it this way:

> *"The first thing our bank does is to look at the character, reputation and past performance of the individual. Character, for me, is honesty and reliability... A person who can't handle his personal finances is unlikely to be much better at business finance."*

Three Different Loans
and How Best to Get Them

Not all loans are alike. There are at least three different types and each must be the focus of your business plan especially if you are approaching a loan officer specifically for that purpose.

Business Expansion Loan: Get a bank loan because you will have property as collateral or capital equipment to secure at least a major portion of the anticipated loan.

Research & Development (R&D) Loan: If your company is trying to get money to finance research and development, a new marketing effort or a new product or process, those loan proceeds will be quickly consumed. Little or no collateral is realized and the traditional bank loan will be difficult to obtain. The best way to go in such a case is through equity funding.

Seasonal Loan: For limited-time money requirements, the traditional bank loan might be too costly. Ask the loan officer for a short-term line of credit. The interest rate is usually lower and collateral requirements easier.

How to Finance Short-Term Debt

Recent interest rates and the realization that if you do borrow, no matter how low the interest, it still costs money, have created a shift in capital borrowing. An accounting firm surveyed a number of businesses to find out how they changed in order to handle cash flow problems in two consecutive fiscal years. While bigger businesses optioned to sell their stock in order to raise capital, smaller firms had more limited options for such capital. Here is how they handled it:

	Year 1	Year 2
Operating profit and company cash flow	64.7%	71.4%
Short-term bank loans	38.2%	58.9%
Long-term bank loans	41.2%	35.7%
Private placements	32.4%	21.4%
Individual lenders	29.4%	12.5%
Public equity capital	5.9%	7.1%
Venture capital	5.9%	5.4%

Raising Capital through the "Other People's Money" Method

If the reason for the "other half" of your business plan is to raise money from other people, then a few words about the *Other People's Money (OPM)* method will be appropriate.

Of course the best way to raise business capital is with your own savings and assets. But if this is not sufficient or is not the way you feel you want to go, then the next "touch" might be your own immediate or even extended family. Even then, if you want to make sure you will remain *persona grata* in your family, you will have to put any family loans or investments on a business-like basis. Your business plan, plus your good family relationships and enthusiasm, will stand you in good stead. Of course, showing that Uncle John can expect some material rewards from your proposal will also cement relationships.

For the sake of this chapter, however, we will look into sources beyond the family or even your own bank account. Here are a few real-life cases that can give you both direction and inspiration.

One man wanted to start a specialty magazine. He figured that it could take as much as $2,000,000 to get it running smoothly. One problem with publication financing always has been that banks consider them almost equivalent to restaurants. They are highly vulnerable; they come and go with regularity. Yet they are glamorous, too, and promoters will always find angels who will support a bright idea. This man had such an idea and a great portfolio of past achievements. He also was a shrewd psychologist, knowing full well that to know who is as important as to know how. He shared his proposal with his fishing buddies and was able to raise more than $600,000 of his capital by casting his bait among his fellow fishermen.

He got fifty investors to participate with $2,000 to $250,000 each by selling convertible debentures that pay regular interest and can be converted into stock. In addition to his fishing buddies, this entrepreneur surveyed managers in the field in which his magazine would be a major player.

Nearly 30 years ago one of the authors of this book followed a similar technique. He invited local people in his immediate area whom he, or his attorney and accountant knew, to a briefing. They were all interested in the product—a newspaper—and a number of them subscribed to investment packages matching his own investment, and thus getting the publication off the ground. It is still being published.

Private placement of loans can also be achieved through advertising for local investors in the business or "business opportunities" columns of the local newspaper. One man raised $700,000 for a real estate development by this method. If you have maintained strong school ties, your ex-college mates might be interested in participating in your venture. Other business people in the community, if they know you and want to see your new venture succeed, are also likely prospects. When a major industry in a town goes bankrupt, the community knits together, especially if a strong Chamber of Commerce gets behind a money-raising drive. "Other people's money" can then be raised rather quickly to prevent local consumers from becoming unemployed and creating a ghost factory or retail building in the town, if the bankrupt business closes shop. In one particular case, state development agencies lent a hand, and between them and numerous investors who were impressed and convinced by the new entrepreneurs' presentation, a large amount was raised just in time to prevent the product line from becoming history.

Other people's money includes venture capital funds. This is a rather tricky and often uncertain source, but if you are going into a fast-track, high-growth product business, and you have a convincing story of high-profit expectations, then venture capitalists will listen to you.

Because of the rather avaricious possibilities of such money lending, it should be approached with caution and knowledge of what you are letting yourself in for. If these money providers guess right, the borrower will get his money along with a lot of advice and supervision, and at the end of a few years—let's say three to five years—the venturers prefer a sellout at a high initial-growth rate. You might not desire to sell, but remember that you have your deal. This is one of the handicaps of other people's money.

It is impossible to overestimate the importance of Know-Who.

OPM can also be Uncle Sam's money, though this source has for some time become harder to get, in direct proportion to the rise of the national debt: the higher the national debt, the tighter government funds have become. Only a small percentage of business loans are guaranteed by the Small Business Administration (SBA), or come from federal agency grants. Yet these sources are not impossible. If you have the patience and know-how, government money should definitely be explored.

The SBA has also made small loan guarantees easier by backing $25,000 requests, relatively small sums, that commercial banks often find unprofitable.

Are you a member of a minority? The government has numerous connections to virtually every federal agency, each of which have a minority office that is set up to help minority enterprises with fiscal and business matters.

It will also be useful to check your State Business Development office, usually located in the state capitol. Many of them have supportive loan programs or can put you in touch with private, state-registered financiers.

Another innovative OPM method of funding is the "Big Brother" method. Example: In Mountain View, California, a small computer company developed a special design application. To market it would take more capital than the firm had available. The owners started their financing search by going for the top: IBM. Their idea and presentation struck a welcome chord in the minds of IBM executives and they agreed not only to finance the small company innovation, but to help in the marketing of it. It was a perfect hand-holding symbiosis that was helped in no small measure by a personal contact at IBM. Again, such OPM financing depended on a combination of *Know-Who* and *Know-How.*

It is impossible to overestimate the importance of *Know-Who*. The latter imparts a degree of credibility that is impossible to obtain otherwise. Another case history to prove this point had its foundation in a Tennessee incubator facility. A young business, a member of this incubator group, needed an infusion of funds for a short period. All attempts to borrow from local banking sources were in vain. Asset-based lenders including banks shied away from the assumed high-risk investment in a small, developing company. But one of the other members of the incubator group had dealt successfully with a bank, and established close rapport with the institution and the county's development center. Literally holding the other business's hand, he took him to the bank and introduced him to the banker, serving also as a needed reference. In short order, the loan was approved—another proof that OPM often starts and ends with other people's influence.

Six Rules to Follow
When You Decide to Borrow Money

1. Bank lenders are like fingerprints. No two are alike, even though their forms are alike. Shop around until your deal and needs dovetail with those of the lender.

2. Know what the lender is looking for: the 4 C's (credit, cash flow, collateral and character). If you come up short on any of them, find another way; ask your mother.

3. There is a right way and a wrong way to borrow. Make sure first of all that the structure of the loan is for your benefit. Then triple-check your application for accuracy and completeness. You cannot look anything less than a professional the first time.

4. If you really know how to structure the deal, you might even borrow 100 percent of the purchase price or need. Read the right books; ask the right people for advice before you hand in that loan application. But remember: the more you borrow, the more you need to prove that you will have the cash flow to pay it back.

5. Don't undervalue yourself; you might be worth more than you think. Research every nook and cranny of your worth. Your own assets might very well cover the down payment or collateral.

6. If you've received your final "no" from a banker, try seller-financing of an existing successful business.

A Short Course in SBA Loan Financing

1. The SBA will consider you for a direct loan only if two banks turn you down. Perhaps if you had prepared your application right the first time, and had the appropriate cash flow, credit and collateral, you wouldn't have to try and cut SBA red tape. Take another look.

2. The SBA requires as much or more collateral as banks, and may include a mortgage on your house.

3. SBA usually wants you to match revenues to show your sincerity and ability to provide adequate collateral; they don't like secondary sources of financing.

4. SBA, as a government agency, works more slowly and the red tape, despite innumerable attempts to streamline procedures, is more pervasive. Will your "deal" wait that long?

5. The SBA tends to favor minority applicants.

6. SBA loans and loan guarantees do have some very real advantages: longer loan payback periods; favored loans in distressed areas; often lower credit rating requirements; favorable considerations of minorities and disadvantaged applicants; a variety of loan programs (more than a thousand!) either within the SBA or with other government agencies (and the SBA can advise you about those other programs).

7. You need to be informed about the loan process and how SBA guarantees loans. Even banking officials do not always have all the necessary information, or simply will not go to the trouble of utilizing the tools that the SBA makes available.

8. You need to be complete, candid, realistic and thorough in writing your Business Plan and loan application.

9. You have to be realistic about your collateral. The latter might have to be from 50 to 100 percent of the loan amount.

10. Because the lender looks primarily at the quality of management and the income generated by a business, as a source of repayment these two factors may be even more important than collateral.

Ten Financing Questions to Ask Yourself:

1. How much do I really need to start my business?

2. How long will it realistically take to break even?

3. How much volume do I need to produce to reach that point?

4. What should my gross and net profit be?

5. What should my fixed and variable expenses be?

6. How do my figures compare with industry figures?

7. Can I adapt this information for my operating budget?

8. Will my business earnings be sufficient to pay off any loan?

9. Can I make adjustments in my budget so I can reach necessary profit goals?

10. Do these figures show that I can develop a profitable business? Or am I premature to gamble my life savings?

Understanding Cash Flow

To be competitive, small business owners must plan and prepare for all future events and market changes. Possibly the most important aspect of preparation is effective cash-flow planning. Failure to properly plan cash flow is one of the leading causes for small business failures in the United States.

In planning and achieving a positive cash flow, you must have a sound plan.
Cash reserves can be increased by:

- Increased sales
  - Price of products or services

- Reduce overall costs
  - Budget your operating expenses
  - Purchase at better prices and longer terms

- Collection of receivables

- Loans, both long-term and short-term

Making a Profit & Loss Statement for your first time
(courtesy of Alex Grossman of SCORE)

The individual who is writing a business plan for the first time is faced with an extremely difficult task when it comes to preparing a Profit & Loss statement for a business that has never been in operation. Typically, many entrepreneurs do not know where to start. It is less difficult to make changes, or corrections of written statement than to make the original working copy.

We (at SCORE) highly recommend that a computer be used in the preparation of your business statements. The advantages of using a computer with a spreadsheet program are tremendous. Use of the computer makes it very easy to make changes, corrections and adjustments to your figures as your statement is developed.

It is absolutely essential that, entering into your new enterprise, you do thorough and comprehensive research on your business endeavor. A good reference library can prove to be extremely helpful to you in obtaining valuable information about typical operating statistics. See page 136 for operating percentages for various businesses. There are three operating percentage figures (ratios) that are most essential to guide you in generating your first P&L statement:

1. Gross Profit on Sales (G/P/S)

2. Gross Operating Expense (GP)

3. Net Income (Net Profit)

These three statistics should be your basic guide in your preparation of your statement for your new businesses first year (take a look at the P&L statement on page 135 to understand the relation between these figures). Armed with your first-year projections, you should then establish a goal for your first *month* of operation. We suggest that you project your operations for the first month to show a Net Profit of 0% (that's ZERO percent). It should be self-evident that the total of your Gross Operating Expenses would then be equal to your Gross Profit (Gross Profit minus

Gross Operating Expense equals Zero Net Profit). In your P&L statements as in all P&L statements, *Gross Sales* minus *Cost of Goods Sold* equals the *Gross Profit on Sales. Gross Profit on Sales* minus *Gross Operating Expense* equals your *Net Profit on Sales.*

Your examination of a typical operating statement in your prospective new enterprise would have revealed the types of expenses that you should account for. (See page 136.) After you've listed all the expense items you should expect, then fill in the dollar amounts you expect to incur during your first month of operation. If you don't expect to incur a particular expense during your first month of operation, then leave the expense item, but place a zero in its cost column. If you feel you can't make an accurate estimate of a specific expense item, then make a reasonable guess.

Add one last expense item to cover expenses you may have overlooked. You should estimate this final item, *Miscellaneous Expense*, as an amount equal to 10% of the total of all your previously-entered *Expenses.*

Make a new total of all your expenses, which you'll call your *Gross Operating Expense.* For example:

My First Month's projected P&L Estimate:
Gross Profit 30%
Gross Operating Expense 30%
Net Profit 0%

Expenses (typical):
Rent $380
Telephone 91
Delivery Expense and Car 150
Salaries and Fringes 1500
Insurance 100
Advertising and Promotion 85
Depreciation 150
Interest 75
Utilities 60
Miscellaneous 259
Total Expense $2850.00

Since you projected the *Gross Profit* to equal the *Gross Operating Expense,* then your projected *Gross Profit* is also $2850. *Gross Profit* divided by .03 (your projected Gross Profit percentage), then your projected sales for the first month's *Sales* is $9500 (that is, $2850 ÷ .30). Put another way, it's necessary for you to produce sales of $9500 in the first month in order to break even.

Your First Month's projected P&L would be:

Sales	$9500	100%
Cost of Goods Sold	6650	70%
Gross Profit	2850	30%
Total Expenses	2850	30%
Net Profit	**$0**	**0%**

Projecting a net profit of zero for the first month provides a quantitative estimate of amount of sales required to break even.

You should examine your first month's projections to make any necessary adjustments. In order to complete your 12-month projection, it's a good idea to project each month individually, thus showing a gradual progression of sales increases. Your projections should be based upon your projection of market conditions and your marketing plan. Using your computer spreadsheet and applying the 30% GP formula, you will quickly obtain the Gross Profit for each month. In a similar manner you will fill in all the projected expenses that your business would incur in each month of operation as sales increase. When you've filled in all the lines, total all your figures both vertically and horizontally. Compute the *percentage of sales* for items on *each line* of your P&L statement. You are now ready to analyze all the figures on your statement to make corrections and adjustments that appear logical, sensible and reachable.

First Month Projected Profit & Loss

Sales . . . . .100.0% $9500

Cost of Good Sold . . . . .70.0% $6650

Gross Profit . . . . .30.0% $2850

Expenses:

    Rent .4.00% $380

    Telephone . . . . .0.96% $91

    Delivery & car expense . . . . . .1.58% $150

    Insurance . . . . .1.05% $100

    Salaries & fringes . . . . .15.79% $1500

    Advertising & promotions . . .0.89% $85

    Depreciation . . . . .1.58% $150

    Interest . . . . .0.79% $75

    Utilities . . . . .0.63% $60

    Miscellaneous expense . . . . . .2.73% $259

Gross Operating expense . . . . . .30.0% $2850

Net Profit . . . . .0.00% $0

Typical Operating Percentage (Ratios) of Doing Business

	C/G/S*	GR/ PROFIT	EXPENSE	NET PROFIT
RETAIL TRADE				
Apparel Store	63.97	36.03	26.54	9.49
Bars, Drinking Place	54.30	45.70	41.20	4.50
Building Material	74.25	25.75	18.69	7.06
Food Store	71.52	28.48	20.34	8.14
Furniture and Home Furn.	67.09	32.91	24.48	8.43
Garden Supply, Nursery	71.60	28.40	24.30	4.10
Gas Station	78.19	21.81	13.89	7.92
General Mdse.	74.89	25.11	18.41	6.70
Gift and Novelty Shop	63.20	36.80	34.00	2.80
Grocery	81.70	18.30	13.89	4.41
Hardware Store	74.80	25.20	20.80	4.40
Liquor Store	82.00	18.00	13.90	4.10
Paint, Glass, Wallpaper	63.90	36.10	28.80	7.30
Restaurants	49.45	50.55	43.57	6.98
Sporting Goods, Bike Shop	69.80	30.20	24.50	5.70
Other Retail Trade	67.30	32.70	27.20	5.50
WHOLESALE TRADE	83.22	16.78	10.79	5.99
RETAIL & WHOLESALE	75.86	24.14	17.63	6.51
MANUFACTURING				
Printing	45.70	54.30	42.20	12.10
CONSTRUCTION				
General Contractor	47.00	53.00	38.00	15.00
Masonry, Plastering	50.94	49.06	31.14	17.92
Painting, Paperhanger	39.97	60.03	33.60	26.43
Plumbing	65.18	34.82	21.56	13.26
SERVICES				
Accounting	1.73	98.27	70.08	28.19
Advertising	42.10	57.90	43.50	14.40
Auto Repair	47.02	52.98	40.14	12.84
Barber Shop	11.50	88.50	59.07	29.43
Beauty Shop	23.00	77.00	57.00	20.00
Building Service	16.00	84.00	51.10	32.90
Dry Clean Services	23.76	76.24	64.86	11.38
Educational Service	23.40	76.60	56.30	20.30
Engineering and Architecture	12.50	87.50	56.40	31.10
Insurance	15.10	84.90	43.10	41.80
Medical and Health Service	7.43	92.57	55.44	37.13
Motel	12.90	87.10	84.40	2.70
Photo Studio	29.00	71.00	54.80	16.20
Repair Service	40.10	59.90	41.30	18.60
TRANSPORTATION	30.85	69.15	68.80	0.35

*C/G/S – Cost of Goods Sold

Index

E

F

I

K

L

M

N

O

P

R

S

T